Edible Pleasures

Lana Citron

Bon Appétit!

First published in 2018
by Eyewear Publishing Ltd
Suite 333, 19-21 Crawford Street
London, W1H 1PJ
United Kingdom

Graphic design by Edwin Smet
Author photograph by Mark Pringle
Cover image A fig plant (Ficus carica): fruiting stem and halved fruit.
Coloured zincograph by J. Macfarlane, c. 1872, after himself.
wellcomecollection.org
Printed in England by TJ International Ltd, Padstow, Cornwall

Set in Bembo 12 / 15 pt
ISBN 978-1-912477-77-7

WWW.EYEWEARPUBLISHING.COM

MIX
Paper from
responsible sources
FSC® C013056

Edible
Pleasures

LANA CITRON

A TEXTBOOK OF APHRODISIACS

 **EYEWEAR** PUBLISHING

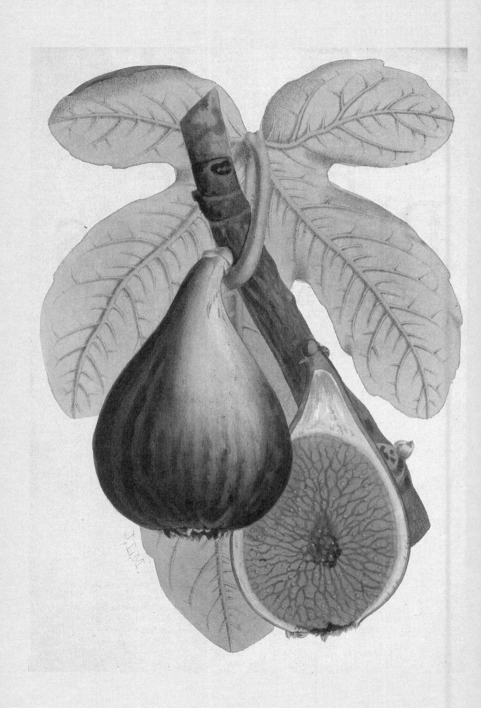

Contents

— Prologue —
A Note From The Author

As often happens in life, one finds oneself on a particular journey by chance, having taken a wrong (or at least unplanned) turn. So it was, a few years ago I came to a dead end and had to change course. Happily, I found myself in a place full of kisses. Yes, kisses. A subject close to my heart, I submerged myself in the world of this extraordinarily potent and most nebulous gesture.

My book *A Compendium of Kisses* was born of that experience. Completely smitten by the breadth and scope of the subject I had stumbled upon, I realized popular perceptions of the kiss were often dismissive, deeming it an adolescent topic or regarding it as a fey gesture, whimsical or, worse still, saccharine.

On the contrary, I discovered that the kiss is fundamental to our very existence, being both life-giving and taking. The shifting status and perception of the kiss throughout history and the myriad meanings attached to it (symbolic, cultural, historical, political and social) is mesmeric.

'The kiss' is a field as yet relatively un-ploughed by historians and academics, especially if one considers that every aspect of Western European life has been kissed, literally and metaphorically.

Whilst writing the *Compendium* I happened upon the following quote and the emotion it conjured struck me:

'I would often ask her,' says Farjeon, *'being of an inquisitive turn of mind,' Mother what have you got for dinner to –day?' 'Bread, Cheese and Kisses,' she would reply merrily. Then I knew that one of our favourite dishes was sure to be on the table and I rejoiced accordingly. And to this day, Bread and Cheese and Kisses bears for me in its simple utterance a scared and beautiful meaning. It means contentment; it means cheerfulness; it means the exercise of sweet works and gentle thought; it means Home!'*[1]

'Bread, Cheese and Kisses' – what more could anybody want? I realized how inextricably entwined kissing and eating were.

Freud conjectured that erotic kissing is a gesture reminiscent to that of being breast-fed.[2]

---

1 C. C. Bombaugh A. M. M. D. *The Literature of Kissing* J. B. Lippincott & Co 1876 p.5
2 Tiefer, Leonore, *The Kiss A 5 0th Anniversary Lecture*, The Kinsey institute Oct 24th 1998

However, there is a significant difference between a child ingesting milk and two adults kissing. The child will eventually be satiated whereas the adult's hunger can only increase; hunger in this case being *desire*.

Yet, when we do kiss, romantically devouring the object of our longing, there is undoubtedly a return to the sensuous primary experience of suckling.

As Adam Philips entertainingly put it: 'If in a crude psychoanalytic interpretation, kissing could be described as aim-inhibited eating, we should also consider the more nonsensical option that eating can also be, as Freud will imply, *aim-inhibited kissing.*'[3]

Aim-inhibited kissing...

If only...!

I fell in love with this idea. That each morsel to touch my lips was a kiss; that I was nourished on love. How romantic! I envisaged gobbling kisses by the jarful, kisses thickly spread on morning toast and crumbs of love falling from chapped lips, my thirst slaked by libidinous liquids...

3 Philips Adam *On kissing, tickling and being bored* Harvard University Press, 1994 p. 97

What better fate than to gorge myself on kisses... then ponder the insatiable hunger that exists in one's belly – and further down![4]

Of course food has long been regarded as an expression of affection, a comfort to the soul, and lovers the world over pass food and drink to one another between kisses. Still, I could not resist the temptation to develop this idea, and from there *Edible Pleasures* has emerged... perhaps an extrapolation too far, but hand on heart, all offered between these pages has either piqued my interest, tickled my fancy or left me wanting.

---

4 Kissing represented as a form of insatiable hunger is a well-versed poetic allegory. The theme of Roman writer Catullus's famous poem, in which he demands hundreds, then thousands of kisses from his lover, is one of gluttonous love,

Kiss me now a
thousand times &
now a hundred
more & then a
hundred & a
thousand more again
till with so many
hundred thousand
kisses you & I
shall both lose count

— Epigram —
The Taste of a Kiss by Martial

Epigram III. 65

The breath of a young girl, biting an apple,

The scent that wafts from Corycian saffron,

The smell of the white vine, flowering with first clusters,

The odour of fresh grass, where sheep have grazed,

Fragrance of myrtle, spice-reaping Arab, rubbed amber,

A fire glowing pale with eastern incense,

The earth just lightly touched with summer rain,

A garland that has circled someone's hair

Wet with spikenard.

Diadumenus, cruel child,

All these things breathe forth from your perfect kisses:

Can you not give them freely, unbegrudging?

PART I

Introduction

Food and love have been synonymous through the ages. The language is analogous, the words entwined, often interchangeable. Love-speak and sweet-talking are full of gastronomic metaphors, epicurean euphemisms and sexual allusions; we crave affection, hunger for love, embark on insatiably romantic quests and devour one another when found. We might describe a woman as a *tart*, *crumpet*, *hot tomato*, *sweetie*, *honey*, *sugar dumpling*, *sweet pea*. A man may be described as *beef cake*, *a dish*, *sugar* daddy, the *apple* of your eye, *tasty*, a veritable *treat*, *eye candy* and so on. How sweet is married life that it begins with a *honeymoon*? When pregnant you have *a bun in the oven*, and when reality hits, you must *earn your daily bread* or your *bread and butter* to prove you are *worth your salt*. These allusions encompass the full descriptive spectrum, from the inspiring to the obscene: there are *codpieces* and *meat and two veg*. Lady Gaga sings 'I'm bluffin, with my muffin', and Kelis's *Milkshake* apparently bring all the boys to the yard. Culture is saturated with such foodie double entendres...

But this is not that sort of book. Instead, here is something from the inspiring end of the spectrum, a poem from 12th century India. [5]

Her breath is like honey spiced with cloves
Her mouth delicious as a ripened mango
To press kisses on her skin is to taste the lotus
The deep cave of her navel shades a store of spices
What pleasure lies beyond the tongue knows
But cannot speak of it.

5 Allende, Isabel Aphrodite, A Memoir of the Senses Flamingo, 1998 p. 7

— The Etymological Essentials —

Appetite – /apItAIt/n. 1. A natural desire to satisfy bodily needs, esp. for food or sexual activity. 2. (usually followed by for) an inclination or desire. [Middle English *apetit*, from Old French, from Latin *appetītus*, strong desire, from past participle of *appetere*, to strive after: ad-, ad- + *petere*, to seek.] ***appetitive*** **ap'pe·ti'tive** (ăp'-tĭ›tĭv, ə-pĕt'ĭ-tĭv) *adj.*

Desire 1. **a** an unsatisfied longing or craving. **b** an expression of this; a request (*expressed a desire to rest*) 2. sexual appetite, lust 3. something desired (*achieved his hearts desire*). • *v.tr* 1. **a** often followed by to + infin., or that + clause) long for, crave **b.** feel sexual desire for. 2. request (*desires a cup of tea*) 3. *archaic* pray entreat or command (*desire him to wait*).[Middle English via Old French *desir*, from *desirer*, from Latin *dēsīderāre* to desire earnestly; see desiderate].

Hunger

n. **a.** A strong desire or need for food. **b.** The discomfort, weakness, or pain caused by a prolonged lack of food. **2.** A strong desire or craving: *a hunger for affection.*

v. **hun·gered, hun·ger·ing, hun·gers** *v.intr.***1.** To have a need or desire for food. **2.** To have a strong desire or craving. *v.tr.* To cause to experience hunger; make hungry.

[Middle English, from Old English *hungor*].

Aphrodisiac [æfrə'dIzIæk]

adj. & *n.* • *adj.* that arouses sexual desire • *noun.* an aphrodisiac drug (Medicine /Pharmacology) or food, etc., that excites sexual desire. [from Greek *aphrodisiakos*, from *aphrodisios* from Aphrodite belonging to the Greek Goddess of Love].

Aphrodite

'For 'twas from the sea, in Cytherean waters, so runs the tale, that the mother of the Amores [Erotes, loves], undraped, arose.'[6]

---

6 Ovid, Heroides 7. 59 ff (trans. Showerman) (Roman poetry C1st B.C. to C1st A.D.)

17

Aphrodite, Greek Goddess of Love and Sexuality was born of sea foam from the mutilated penis of Uranus after he had been dethroned by his son Cronus.[7]

Known as Venus by the Romans, Aphrodite was worshipped as a goddess of sex, love, seduction, beauty, pleasure and happiness. Linked to food from the start, an Orphic Ode described her as the, 'patroness of the feasts which last for nights'.[8]

---

7 'Ouranos (the Sky) came, bringing on night and longing for love, and he lay about Gaia (the Earth) spreading himself full upon her. Then the son [Kronos] from his ambush stretched forth his left hand and in his right took the great long sickle with jagged teeth, and swiftly lopped off his own father's members and... cast them from the land into the surging sea, and a white foam spread around them from the immortal flesh, and in it there grew a maiden... an awful and lovely goddess... Her gods and men call Aphrodite, Hesiod, Theogony 176 ff (trans. Evelyn-White) (Greek epic C8th or 7th B.C.)

8 Hospodar Miriam Aphrodisiac Foods Bringing Heaven to Earth Gastronomica – The Journal of Food and Culture, Vol 4 No, 4 p. 83-93

— Desire, Passion And The Pursuit Of Oral Pleasure —

*It seems to me that our three basic needs for food and secu-
rity and love, are so mixed and mingled and entwined...
– that when I write of hunger, I am really writing about
love and the hunger for it, and warmth and the love of
it and the hunger for it; and then the warmth and rich-
ness and fine reality of hunger satisfied; and it is all one.*
– M.F.K. Fisher, The Art of Eating

Hungry for Love

From fertility rituals, ancient Roman orgiastic
feasts, nude dining popular in medieval times to
the (perhaps more prosaic) romantic meal down
at the local bistro, sexual hunger and physical
hunger have always been allies.

Our relationship with food exceeds simple
nutritional sustenance and is of immense importance throughout our lives, emotionally, psycho-
logically and spiritually. Sharing a meal is basic
human behaviour and a primary commandment
of every seducer's manual. This link between

food and sex is relatively easy to understand and is put succinctly by Freud:

> *No one who has seen a baby sinking back satiated from the breast and falling asleep with flushed cheeks and a blissful smile can escape the reflection that this picture persists as a prototype of the expression of sexual satisfaction in later life.*
>
> – Sigmund Freud, *Three Essays on Sexuality* (1905)

Ultimately, food represents life, or the essence of life. There is a longstanding human quest to discover the mystery of creation and consequently how life might be prolonged[9]. Until recent times people had a limited life expectancy. A couple of hundred years ago most would only reach the age of thirty-five. Many women died in childbirth so one had far less time to go forth and multiply.

Creation and reproduction were regarded as inextricably connected to nature. The earth yielded sustenance, in effect giving birth to food. There are many incidences of early rural societies involving ritual intercourse around harvest time and also prior to planting – 'seeds were enriched by the effluvia of human sex.'[10] As Diane Acker-

---

9 Hospodar, Miriam *Aphrodisiac Foods, Bringing Heaven to Earth* Gastronomica, the Journal of Food and Culture Vol.4 P82

10 Ekdah, Raviez Marilyn, *Erotic Cuisine, A Natural History of Aphrodisiac Cookery* Xlibrus Corporation, 2000. P17-18

man elaborates in her book, A Natural History of the Senses, 'when we eat an apple or peach we are eating the fruit's placenta'.[11]

It was believed that certain bodily fluids had life-giving power, especially semen[12], and as such, have been time-honoured ingredients in aphrodisiacs.

Coffee, anyone?

A Brazilian custom exists where in order to attain the object of their desire, women offer them a coffee made by straining the liquid through their dirty underclothing. A similar confection cooked up by Voodoo priestesses to enslave a maiden's intended, mixes a woman's urine, underarm sweat and vaginal secretions into coffee.

Ancient Greek courtesans perfumed their breath and erogenous zones with a blend of violets and their own natural perspiration and secretions, which would 'alleviate (s) the melancholia of the eldest men and torment (s) the young beyond endurance.' [13]

---

11 Ackerman, Diane A Natural History of the Senses Phoenix Paperback 1996, p. 132
12 Until 1845 when the female reproductive system was fully understood, many Europeans believed sperm contained a homunculus, or fully developed miniature human being. Hospodar, Miriam Aphrodisiac Foods, Bringing Heaven to Earth Gastronomica, the Journal of Food and Culture Vol.4, p. 90
13 Allende, Isabel Aphrodite, A Memoir of the Senses Flamingo 1998, p. 10

Besides the use of such secretions, food can also take on a sexual form. Modern day chocolate penises are bland compared to ancient fertility rituals, which included baked meats and breads in the shape of genitals, especially penises. Romans employed *hetaerae* (sacred prostitutes) to bake male and female genital shaped breads. The Latin word for oven – *forno* – is derived from the word 'fornicate.'[14]

In his 21 volume *Decretal of Church Morality*, the German Bishop Burchard of Worms (950-1025) decried the behaviour of certain citizens in his parish:

> Have you done what certain women are in the habit of doing? They prostrate themselves face downwards, rump upward and uncovered have a loaf of bread kneaded upon their nude nates; when it has been baked, they invite their husbands to come and eat it; this they do in order to inflame their men.[15]

At the most fundamental level, food provides energy, fuel to drive our passions. In the words of the famous French chef Grimod de la Reyniere, 'there are two essentials for a love-nest, a stove and mattress.'

---

14 Hospodar, Miriam *Aphrodisiac Foods, Bringing Heaven to Earth* Gastronomica, the Journal of Food and Culture Vol.4, p. 86

15 ibid

Divine Sustenance

Food is of spiritual importance in all cultures and religions. From births, christenings, bar mitzvahs, to birthdays, weddings and wakes – all of life's rites of passage involve the sharing of food to sanctify, mark and celebrate the event. It is during such festivities that cultural beliefs concerning food and sex are revealed.

The Greeks revered Mother Nature, the goddess Gaia. Zeus and his cohorts were represented as millers, their consorts' mills thus baking humans into existence. Ancient Egyptians were of the belief that onions symbolised the many layered universe and swore oaths upon the vegetable as one does upon a sacred bible. When Catholics and Anglicans receive the Eucharist, they ingest godly substances. Jesus appealed to his followers:

> Take, eat, this is my body... Take, drink, this is my blood... Do this in remembrance of me.

Jews eat bitter herbs at Passover in memory of their enslavement in Egypt and have all but patented chicken soup as a panacea for life's ills. During the month of Ramadan, Muslims fast from dawn to dusk to purify the soul, re-focus attention on God, and practice self-sacrifice.

Even when we leave this earthly realm and our spirits journey forth, we are enticed further by the promise of food. There is the milk and honey of the Promised Land, Valhalla mead from the Nordic heavenly hemisphere, intoxicating soma brewed in the Nirvana of the Hindu and, if we should find ourselves in the company of Zeus on Mount Olympus, we would no doubt raise a glass of nectar and ambrosia to our good fortune. In one form of Paradise, men will be rewarded with wine forbidden to them whilst on earth and attended by Houris, bright-eyed maidens who remain virgins no matter how many times men make love to them.[16]

---

16 Parrinder , G, *Sex in the World's Great Religions* Toronto: General Publishing, 1980, p. 170

— On How An Appetite Is Formed —

The very notion of eating (like kissing!) involves all our senses: touch, taste, sight, smell and sound – all elements that contribute to our enjoyment of consummation. So, before we go any further it is only appropriate that we should explore the more sensory mechanics of eating.

Good Taste

> Good taste is the excuse I have given for leading such a bad life.
> – Oscar Wilde

What we colloquially call 'taste' are the oral sensations encountered from eating and drinking. What we sense are the textures, temperature and most importantly the smell of the food and drink.

There are five basic taste sensations: **salt**, **sour**, **sweet**, **bitter** and the most recently discovered, **'umami.'** Umami was pinpointed by Japanese scientist Kikunae Ikeda in the early 1900s, (and ignored by the West for most of the twentieth century). It translates as 'deliciousness' or 'savoury' and has been described as the taste of pure protein. It is common in Japanese foods, particularly kombu, a type of sea vegetable similar to kelp, and in bacon and monosodium glutamate (MSG). There is considerable debate about the existence of a sixth taste receptor for fat.

The Geography of the Tasting Tongue

When we journey over the tongue, we first taste **sweetness,** which is found at the tip of the tongue. A sweet taste signals carbohydrates. **Sour** tasting buds are found on the periphery of the tongue as if aware they are an acquired taste.

Salt receptors are scattered over the surface of the tongue, mainly up front. Besides making food taste better, salt is part of us and we need it to survive. Our blood, sweat and tears taste salty because salt seasons all of our bodily fluids. If we didn't consume salt we would die, as was the fate of thousands of Napoleon's troops during his retreat from Moscow. Their wounds could not heal as a result of a lack of salt in their diet.[17]

---

17 Herz, Rachel *The Scent of Desire* William Morrow 2007, p. 193

Bitterness hangs at the back of our throats. Bitter things tend to be poisonous. Household detergents for example are deliberately acrid, so we will spit them out. But some bitter compounds found in vegetables are extremely healthful, particularly in reducing the risk of cancer; especially cruciferous vegetables such as horseradish, rocket, broccoli and kale.

Most people assume that our sense of taste is restricted to the tongue but you actually taste with your whole mouth. The subtleties in flavour are released when taste buds with saliva liquefies food. There are also incidental taste buds on the palate, pharynx and tonsils. Gastronome extraordinaire, Brillat Savarin and author of *The Physiology of Taste*, recounts the story of a visit to Algeria where he encountered a Frenchman who had had his tongue cut out yet could still taste fairly well, 'but very bitter or sour things caused him unbearable pain.'

Taste buds are located in small pits and grooves called papilla, which are visible to the eye and oft mistaken for taste buds. Each papilla has an average of about six buds in it, which in turn contain forty to sixty cells arranged in segments like an orange. Babies have more taste buds then adults with some spotted inside their cheeks. In total adults have approximately 10,000 taste buds with only half allotted to the tongue. In comparison to humans, rabbits have 17,000, parrots 400 and cows 25,000. Butterflies and blowflies have most of their taste organs on their front feet and need only step in a sweet solution to taste it.[18] The average lifespan of a taste bud is a week to ten days and then they replace themselves. However, this self-replacement decreases with age, so our palates really do become jaded.

Tasting good enough to eat...

Everything else one deems 'taste' is in fact 'smell'. To illustrate, it takes 25,000 times more molecules of cherry pie to taste it than to smell it.[19]

One of the major features that differentiates our sense of taste from our sense of smell is that our responses to taste are primarily hardwired and innate rather than learned as they are with scents. A baby will smile and grimace depending on if she tastes something sweet or sour.

---

18 Ackerman, Diane *A Natural History of the Senses* Phoenix Paperback 1996, p. 138 – 139
19 Ibid., p. 142

...smell and taste are in fact but a single composite sense, whose laboratory is the mouth and its chimney the nose...
– Anthelme Brillat-Savarin

As you eat, you smell your food twice, once through your nose as food approaches your mouth (called *orthonasal olfaction*) and again when the food is in your mouth (liquefied food moves up behind the roof of the mouth in the nasal cavity). Our brains trick us by seamlessly knitting together the sensation of taste and smell and give us the flavours that make up our food world.

Love's Flavour...
A flavour is simply an aroma that you eat. All flavours are chemical and most are manufactured. The world's largest flavour and fragrance company, Givaudan, makes 6,000 versions of strawberry flavour alone.

In the Middle Ages, food was not particularly palatable. Meat was preserved with salt and then cooked. When Marco Polo returned from Asia with spices he revolutionised both the culinary and social order. The value of spices was on a par with gold. A pound of ginger could cost the buyer a sheep. In the first century A.D., Pliny the Elder wrote that 350 grams of cinnamon was of equal value to five kilograms of silver, about fifteen times the value of silver per weight.[20] Pepper was worth more than gold and Arab traders sold it by the peppercorn. Over time, this value diminished and in legal parlance the fee of a peppercorn is used as a metaphor for a very small payment or nominal consideration.

The Scent of Love

> Woman is like a fruit which will only yield its fragrances when rubbed by the hands. Take for example the basil: unless it be warmed by the fingers it emits no perfume... the same with women: if you do not animate her with your frolics and kisses, with nibbling of her thighs and close embraces, you will not obtain what you desire: you will experience no pleasure when she shares your couch and she will feel no affection for you.[21]

From an evolutionary viewpoint, the olfactory sense (sense of smell) is our oldest. We identify things by their perfume. Smell is more intensely and intimately linked to our moods and emo-

---

20 Peggy Trowbridge Filippone in Cinnamon History on About.com
21 Burton, Sir Richard Shaykh Nefzawi's *The Perfumed Garden*, p. 188

tional life than any of our other sensory experiences. One waft and memories may be reawakened, transporting one back to a particular place in time.

Of all the literary greats, Proust is perhaps the most famous for his olfactory sense recollection. The aroma arising from a Madeleine pastry soaked in a cup of linden tea was enough to inspire his masterpiece, *A La Recherche du Temps Perdu*.

> No sooner had the warm liquid, and the crumbs with it, touched my palate than a shudder ran through my whole body, and I stopped, intent upon the extraordinary changes that were taking place. An exquisite pleasure had invaded my senses, but individual, detached with no suggestion of its origin... Whence could it have come to me, this all powerful joy? I was conscious that it was connected with the taste of the tea and cake but that it infinitely transcended those savors.[22]

---

22 Proust, Marcel *Swann's Way*, The Modern Library New York, 1928, p. 62

Madeleine

Ingredients

Two large eggs, lightly beaten

2/3 cups sugar

1 cup of flour

Drops of lemon juice and vanilla[23]

5 oz. butter

Pinch of salt

Zest of 1 lemon

Method

Preheat the oven to 375 degrees Fahrenheit. Measure 1/4 c. eggs into bowl. Beat in sugar and flour. Blend and allow resting for 10 minutes. Meanwhile: Melt butter in saucepan. Bring to a boil and let brown slightly, (it should be a lovely caramel colour). Place 1 1/2 T. in a bowl and set aside (very important!) Stir the rest of the butter over ice until cool but still liquid.

Blend the cooled butter with the reserved 1/4 c. of the eggs into the butter with the salt, lemon juice, rind and vanilla. Mix remaining butter (1T) with the 1T of flour you have reserved, and use the mixture to prepare the Madeleine pans. Bake 13-15 minutes or until browned around the edges and a teensy bit on top.

---

23 Child, Julia *The Way to Cook* Knopf, 1993

Sniffing between the lines

The pages of literature are steeped in odours. James Joyce tells us Leopold Bloom:

> ... ate with relish the inner organs of beasts and fowls; he liked thick giblet soup, nutty gizzards, a stuffed roast heart, liver slices fried with crustcrumbs, fried hencods' roes. Most of all he liked grilled mutton kidneys which gave to his palate a fine tang of faint scented urine.

In Peter Suskind's novel *Perfume*, the anti-hero Jean-Baptiste Grenouille is born without his own smell, otherwise known as his 'unique set of MHC genes' (major histocompatibility complex) or 'individual smell prints'.

Grenouille longs to be accepted into a scented society but is thwarted by his lack of primal essence.

The success of the novel was due in part to exquisite descriptions of smells; for example, Grenouille can smell the mood of the cow from his daily glass of milk. Accompanying the release of the movie adaptation was a coffret of 14 scents replicating Grenouilles' world.

The perfumes on offer included 'Baby', a sweet-sour milky concoction with notes of heavy whipped cream, meringue, fine custard, brown sugar, caramel and butter. 'Paris 1738' was designed to evoke the street smells of the period and 'Virgin No.1' is said to capture the scent of a pubescent girl.[24]

In the most scent-drenched poem of all time *The Song of Solomon* (a book of the Hebrew Bible), the King tells his beloved that on their wedding night, he will 'enter her garden', and catalogues the fruits and spices he knows he will find there: frankincense, myrrh saffron, nard, camphire, pomegranates, aloes, cinnamon, calamus and other treasures. So stirred by his sensuous words and wild with desire she replies:

> Awake O north wind and come thou south blow upon my garden that the spices thereof may flow out, let my beloved come into his garden and eat his pleasant fruits...

The Science of Smell

The area of the brain that processes smell is intertwined with the area that processes emotions. Smell and emotion are located in the same network of neural structures called the Limbic system. This system is the ancient core of the brain

---

24 http://www.basenotes.net/content/153-The-smell-of-flesh-life-and-death-Perfume-The-Coffret-of-the-Senses

– sometimes called the reptilian brain because we share it with reptiles. Its other name is the rhinencephalon, literally the 'nose brain.'[25]

Amorous desire begins in the nose. Alchemy between people arises due to pheromones. A pheromone, from the Greek *pherein* (to carry) and *horman* (to excite), is a chemical substance produced by animals (including humans), which cause a reaction in another, usually of the same species. They are powerful chemical means of communicating.

Scent & Sensuality

The perfumes of good cooking make us salivate and crave in a way that is, if not erotic, then closely related to it. [26] In France, the mix of intimate aromas a woman exudes is called her 'cassolette'. In some Asian countries such as Borneo, Burma and India, the word 'kiss' means smell. In 16th century England, paramours exchanged love apples, where a woman would keep a peeled apple in her armpit until it was saturated with her sweat and then give it to her sweetheart as a scent token.[27]

---

25 Herz, Rachel *The Scent of Desire* William Morrow 2007, p. 197

26 Ekdah, Raviez Marilyn, Erotic Cuisine, A Natural History of Aphrodisiac Cookery Xlibrus Corporation, 2000, p. 52

27 Herz, Rachel *The Scent of Desire* William Morrow 2007, p. 119

These women behind the store windows? Dreams, sir, dreams at bargain prices, a trip to the Indies! These people perfume themselves with spices. You enter, they close the curtains, and the trip begins. The gods descend on the nude bodies and the islands drift, demented, with the tousled hair of palm trees in the breeze.

– Albert Camus, The Fall (1956)

My Eau du You

Smell is our most sexual of senses. As such, our smell print is vital to our sexuality and reproductive success. It has been found that to ensure one's offspring has the optimum genetic makeup, women use smell to identify men with opposite immune system proteins to their own.[28]

Having children with someone who has a genetically similar immune system as yours, doubles your child's chance of receiving recessive traits. This harkens back to evolutionary biology, as women invest far more than men do in bearing a child and have thus developed a heightened sense of taste and smell to men. (This has been borne out by scientific studies, where smell was less important for men.)[29]

---

28 The reason a male commits to a particular partner is to ensure that the child born is his. Genetic testing is a relatively recent scientific discovery thus a man was dependent on a woman's honesty to know whether a child was his or not.

29 Herz, Rachel The Scent of Desire William Morrow 2007, p. 128-129

Claus Wedekind, a Swiss zoologist at the University of Bern, tested the theory that women choose men as sexual partners on the basis of their body odour and the chemistry created, and found it to be true.

However, there was one proviso: it only worked on women who were not taking the birth control pill, as those who were tended to select men with the most genetically similar traits to them. This was because the pill hormonally mimics the state of pregnancy and during pregnancy, a woman feels vulnerable and so feels safest with family rather than a stranger.

Whether or not aromatic aphrodisiacs actually work is still debated; certainly it is a subject which has obsessed scientists and lovers alike for centuries, something which accounts for the huge market in commercial scents chemically styled to attract the other sex.

The Smell of Ages

The Greeks employed scents for amorous dalliance as well as health maintenance, and records suggest that Athens was full of perfume shops. Cleopatra drenched the sails of her gilded barges with the fragrance of the Damascus rose. Indeed, throughout history, floors have been strewn with rose petals and rooms perfumed by slaves blowing sweet attars (essential oils) through ingenious silver tubes. The Romans imported boatloads of flowers for floor covering, and during lavish feasts dropped them over diners from trick ceilings.[30]

Even in Medieval times, floors were covered with straw, aromatic herbs and petals to mask the stench of garbage and excrement. Before Thomas Crapper's life-changing invention, the flushing lavatory, both nobles and lackeys took relief behind the draperies.

In Louis XV's perfumed court, servants used to drench doves in different scents and release them at dinner parties to weave a tapestry of aromas as they flew around the guests. With the discovery of new and exotic scents from Asia and America, the 17th and 18th centuries became known as 'the age of the European perfumery'; that one's perfume dictated ones' status shows the extent to which this was the case. In 1709, a French perfumer proposed that the different classes should each have a special scent. He con-

30 When Romans discussed important private matters, they placed a vase of roses on the table. Whatever was communicated thus was sub *Rosa* (under the rose) or in the strictest confidence, a practice said to evolve from the legend that Cupid gave Harpocrates, the God of Silence, a rose as a bribe to hush up the love affairs of Venus. Hendrickson, Robert *Lewd Food: The Complete Guide to Aphrodisiac Edibles* Chilton Book Company, 1974, p. 269

cocted a royal perfume for the aristocracy and a bourgeois perfume for the middle classes. But the poor were only deemed worthy of disinfectant.[31]

George Orwell echoed this thought: 'the lower classes smell... [N]o feeling of like or dislike is quite so fundamental as a physical feeling... You can have an affection for a murderer or a sodomite, but you cannot have an affection for a man whose breath stinks.'[32]

Scent, Lust and Food

The entwining of scent, lust and food is famously evoked in Mexican author Laura Esquivel's novel, *Like Water for Chocolate*. The heroine, Tita, is forced to cook the marriage banquet of her true love Pedro – unfortunately betrothed to her own sister. Tita succeeds in imbuing the wedding cake with such longing that it causes the guests to wander off and seek desperate relief. Later, Tita is given a bouquet of roses by Pedro, now her brother-in-law. She uses the petals to create, 'Quail in Rose Petal Sauce.' This dish so impassions the diners that Tita's sister Gertrudis leaves to cool off with a shower...

---

31 Herz, Rachel *The Scent of Desire* William Morrow 2007, p. 173
32 Orwell George *The Road to Wigan Pier*, chapter 8

Should you wish to exude the scent of roses as Gertrudis does and perhaps find your self being swept up in the arms of a wandering revolutionary soldier, this may be worth trying...

Quail in Rose Petal Sauce

Ingredients

6 Quails	2 Tablespoons cornstarch
12 Roses (red, preferably)	2 Drops rose essence
12 Almonds, toasted	2 Tablespoons star anise
Butter	2 Tablespoons honey
2 Cloves of garlic	Salt and pepper

Method

Carefully separate the rose petals. Grind them in a mortar with the anise. Cook the almonds in water and purée them. Mince the garlic and sweat them in butter. Add the almond purée, honey, rose petal mixture and salt. If necessary, add the cornstarch to adjust thickness. Add the rose essence. Place the quails in the sauce and simmer them for a maximum of ten minutes so they'll take the flavor. According to the book, they are to be served in a platter with a whole rose in the center and petals scattered around.

A Pinch of Floral Essences

Flowers have always been used to scent dishes, especially cakes and pastries. Jules Maincave, an innovative French chef who died in the WW1 trenches advocated resurrecting the use of flowers to flavour entrées and savoury dishes. *'I think nothing is more exquisite than beef in Kummel, garnished with slices of banana stuffed with Gruyère or pureed sardines with Camembert or whipped cream with tomato sprinkled with brandy or a chicken with lily of the valley.'*[33] The Heston Blumenthal of his day, another of Maincave's recipes included peanut butter and jelly soup.

Recently food scents such as vanilla, fig, citrus and cinnamon have become hugely popular in skin creams, lotions, balms, shampoos and perfumes. A more acquired taste (or should that be 'scent') would be Eau de Stilton created by the English Stilton Cheese Makers Association in 2006. The perfume, described as 'fruity and earthy,' received something of a mixed reaction when launched.[34]

---

33 Chef Jules Maincave (1910) quoted in 'Larousse Gastronomique'
34 Stilton scent pleases cheese fans http://news.bbc.co.uk/1/hi/england/leicester-shire/4761989.stm

A Scentual (sic) Meal for Two
(An idea not to be sniffed at!)

For those with a nose for love there follows the description of a most fragrant 'dinner a deux' presented by a grand seducer to his beloved.

We are told the first course consisted of a single carnation served on a silver platter; the second, a bunch of roses, came on a gold platter. A large magnolia floating on water in a cut crystal bowl arrived next, and then came a forth course consisting of pom-pom dahlias, chased by a spray of tiger lilies. The meal ended with the delicate intake of the scent of violets.[35]

Touch
Bonding by touch commences at childbirth and continues throughout life. Touching those we like or love elevates the production of endorphins, in particular the production of oxytocin, which enhances bonding and commitment.

When considering the sense of touch in the context of food, there is of course the touch and texture of the foodstuff on skin, tongue, teeth and lips. But one must also bear in mind the re-

---

35 Hendrickson, Robert *Lewd Food: The Complete Guide to Aphrodisiac Edibles* Chilton Book Company, 1974, p. 259

ceptacles and cutlery, the purpose of which is to present food, and then shape and transport it to the mouth.

Sound

The potential influence of sound is obvious. Sounds subtly enhance and create a mood. The perfect soundtrack to a grand seduction may include the sizzling and crackling sounds of the stove, the uncorking of a bottle of fine wine, (although twist caps have of late silenced that pleasure), the tinkle of glass, the crack of nuts, and the faint hiss and flicker of candles.

Vision

As a sense, vision offers enormous arousal potential. Stimuli include the food's presentation, the freshness of natural ingredients, and our own personal appearance. The room setting, dimmed lights etc, all contribute to a seductive ambiance, but perhaps the most primal atmospheric aphrodisiac of all is firelight. Since its discovery, the controlled use of fire has signified family, safety, rest, commensality (the act of eating together) – and imminent sexual activity.

The Aesthetics of Food

The relationship between aesthetics and food has been widely celebrated over time. Food is depicted in all facets of culture: painting, literature, film and music.

Tommaso Marinetti, founder of the Italian Futurist Party (later absorbed into the Fascist party), wrote *The Futurist Cookbook* (1932) in which he stated that foods have colours, which are evocative of emotions, sexuality and so forth.

This cookbook contained the most extraordinary recipes and has both delighted and mystified gastronomists:[36]

Aerofood: This signature Futurist dish had a strong tactile element. Whilst being blasted with a giant fan (preferably an airplane propeller) the diner was instructed to eat pieces of olive, fennel, and kumquat with the right hand and to caress various swatches of sandpaper, velvet, and silk with the left. Accompanied by the strains of a Wagner opera the diner is also sprayed with the scent of carnations. ('Astonishing results,' Marinetti says. 'Test them and see.')

---

36 Tommaso Marinetti (translated by Suzanne Brill) *The Futurist Cookbook* Trefoil Publications Ltd © 1989

Italian Breasts in the Sunshine: This dish is described as two half spheres of almond paste, with a fresh strawberry at the centre of each, sprinkled with black pepper.

The Regenerator: A formula by the Futurist engineer Barosi, this dish includes an egg yolk beaten with half a glass of Asti Spumante, 3 roasted nuts, 3 teaspoons of sugar. Serve in a glass with a peeled banana sticking out of it.

Beautiful Nude Food Portrait: Fill a crystal bowl with fresh milk and the flesh of two boiled capons, then scatter with violet petals.

Equator & North Pole: An equatorial sea of golden poached egg yokes surrounds a cone made of whipped egg whites. This is dotted with orange segments like succulent pieces of the sun and black truffle carved to look like airplanes.

Diabolical Roses: Red roses, battered and deep-fried.

Salvador Dalí was strongly influenced by Marinetti. In his cookbook *Les Diners de Gala*, Dali provided recipes for a Venus de Milo made from hard-boiled eggs ('imagine the pleasure', he explained, 'of biting into her yolky breast'). His surrealist paintings included food imagery, such as 'Average French Bread with Two Fried Eggs without the Plate Trying to Sodomize a Crumb of Portuguese Bread' (1932).

In the modern world, Dalí declared, 'beauty will be edible or not at all.'[37]

Etiquette

The human penchant for rituals is deeply seated. It permeates human neurology and we are literately coded for ritual behaviours. Eating together is pleasurable and results in profound sensual satisfactions. The breaking of bread and sharing of salt signals the suspension of hostility and the affirmations of shared humanity. The lonely diner evokes a kind of sadness. [38]

Dining rules and the aesthetics for etiquette change over time but their presence is constant. Egyptians ate sitting and with both sexes pres-

---

37 Irwin, Robert, "The Disgusting Dinners of Salvador Dali," Proceedings of the Oxford Symposium on Food and Cookery, 1998, p. 103-111

38 Ekdah, Raviez Marilyn, *Erotic Cuisine, A Natural History of Aphrodisiac Cookery* Xlibrus Corporation, 2000, p. 23

ent, whilst the Greeks dined reclining and usually segregated by sex. Arabs burp loudly to signal contentment and Indians eat with the fingers of their right hand.

The ancient Romans held the most lavish gastronomic orgies imaginable. There were no moral or culinary boundaries to detract from their pursuit of pleasure as evidenced from descriptions of the most sumptuous, ingenious, bacchanalian feasts. Everything was done to excess, from the food presentation (animals stuffed within other animals or trompes d'oeil) to the entertainment: acrobats, prostitutes (there for the taking), gladiators fighting to the death atop tables (a more vigorous type of table top dancing) not to forget the midgets, handicapped and deformed, on view to be ridiculed.

It was a period when life was of little or no value if born into the wrong milieu. Torture and maltreatment was socially acceptable. Consequently, it is hardly surprising that Christianity arose as a slave class movement, emphasising self-denial and restraint. The message was clear: the poor would inherit the earth, finally giving some hope to the miserable lives of the masses. Christianity offered a rich and free afterlife to the believer.

In contrast, the rich were damned to an eternity of torture. Thus, pleasure became synonymous with guilt and with Hell – and by default even more deliciously tempting...

Table Manners

By the 13th century in Europe a book had been penned which defined appropriate conduct when dining. The *Courtesies of the Table* dictated: 'Do not fill your mouth too full: the glutton who fills his mouth will not be able to reply when spoken to. Those taking soup do not swallow your spoons (sic). Let the hand be clean', and above all 'do not at table scratch your head nor indeed any portion of your body'.[39]

The Perfect Situation

For complete abandonment without shame or reserve, the Indian sex manual (written in 15th/16th century), *The Ananga Ranga* describes the best situation for making love as a large, airy room with musical instruments and refreshments of cocoa nut, betel leaf and milk, 'which is useful for retaining and restoring vigor.' Wall lights 'should gleam, reflected by mirrors.' Thus, the scene is set...

---

39 Ekdah, Raviez Marilyn, *Erotic Cuisine, A Natural History of Aphrodisiac Cookery* Xlibrus Corporation, 2000, p. 25

In summation, according to Brillat-Savarin in *The Physiology of Taste* the senses are the means by which man communicates with the world outside himself.

sight, which embraces the space itself, and tells us by means of light of the existence of the objects, which surround us, and of their colours.

hearing, which absorbs through the air the vibrations caused by agreeably resonant or merely noisy bodies.

smell, the means by which we savour all odorous things.

taste, by which we appreciate whatever is palatable or only edible.

touch, by which we are made aware of the surfaces and textures of objects.

Finally, **physical desire**, which draws the two sexes together so that they may procreate.

'After dining... In this state an unfamiliar languor creeps over him, objects fade, and his body grows limp... When he awakens a secret fire burns in his breast, a new organ had been developed he feels that now he must share his life with someone... This active, troubling imperious sentiment is common to both sexes; it brings them together and unites them, and when the germ of a new life has been fertilized the two people can sleep again in peace they had fulfilled the most sacred of their duties in thus making sure that mankind will continue.' [40]

---

40 Brillat-Savarin, Jean Anthelme *The Physiology of Taste* (translated by M.F.K. Fisher) Everymans Library, 2009, p. 42-43

PART II

— Edible Pleasures —

Aphrodisiacs

The sole love potion I ever used was kissing and embracing, by which alone I made men rave like beasts and compelled them to worship me as an idol.
– Lucretia, 6th century

There is no stronger aphrodisiacal stimulant than the desire provoked by one's own mind; man's foremost erogenous zone. Yet, since time immemorial humankind has used innumerable amatory aids (edible or otherwise), in an attempt to stoke the flames of sexual longing and arousal, as well as to entice, seduce and even entrap the object of one's lust. As Ovid states soberly in the *Art of Love*, ' [love] *will not come to you gliding through the yielding air: the fair one that suits must be sought.*' And if one is lucky to have found a love everlasting, then such stimulants may be used to provoke, prolong and enhance sexual performance.

Types

The use of food to heighten sexual experience is a universal trait found throughout history regardless of culture. Whether aphrodisiacs actually work is harder to verify scientifically.

Ingestible aphrodisiacs fall into the following categories:

Biochemical aphrodisiacs have a direct effect on sexual activity, i.e. *asparagines* and *aspartic acid* found in asparagus act as diuretics, and phosphorus found in fish has an effect on the genito-urinary tract. Foods rich in specific vitamins are considered aphrodisiacal, the most potent vitamins being: D, which is said to increase sexual drive; E, known as the sexuality vitamin; A, supplies nourishment to mucous membranes; and B, which deals with the sexual functioning of the pituitary gland.[41]

Medical Aphrodisiacs are those prescribed in aid of virility, fertility and sexual pleasure. Such aphrodisiacs, prominent in the ancient medical systems of Asia, Egypt, and the Middle East, were

---

41 Hendrickson, Robert *Lewd Food: The Complete Guide to Aphrodisiac Edibles* Chilton Book Company, 1974, p. 14

incorporated into the medicine of Ancient Greece and Rome, which in turn formed the basis of renaissance European medicine. The central idea was that that all forms of life possess 'humours' (vital qualities, life force or 'chi', as Taoists would put it.)

One's 'humour' was hot, cold, moist or dry. Physicians treated diseases with medicines that had opposite qualities, for example such as prescribing a cold herb to cure a hot disease.

Psycho-physiological Aphrodisiacs refer to foods that bear visual and/or tactile resemblances to sexual objects, all stemming from a medieval philosophy known as the *'Doctrine of Signatures'*.

People believed that God designated his purpose for things by their appearance; for example, if the purpose of an herb was to treat the liver, then it would resemble a liver. Thus, some herbs and plants were labeled aphrodisiacs because they resembled genitalia. Various fruits famously resemble male and female genitalia, notably the banana, cucumber, peach, vanilla sheath and melon. Another obvious example is the oyster: in its shell it resembles the male testes and unshelled, the female vulva. Also included here are those aphrodisiacs which work by association: caviar, or the musky smell of truffles, which both evoke an erotic response.

The Law of Similars, so called in *The Golden Bough* by James Frazer, refers to the belief that people could imbibe vitality, strength or vigour by ingesting vital organs, genitals or the blood of specific animals, for example tiger's testes, snakes' blood and brains. The potency of these aphrodisiacs is implicit. Dried testicles of deer, tiger, seal and beaver were used in Chinese sex tonics. The spotted gecko, which mates for a full day, is literally caught in the act, dried and soaked in wine.[42]

The ancient Indian medical text *Characka Samhita* advocates the following:

'If one is saturated with cock's meat fried in crocodile semen he does not sleep at night and has penis ever stiffened.'

---

42 Hospodar, Miriam *Aphrodisiac Foods, Bringing Heaven to Earth* Gastronomica, the Journal of Food and Culture Vol.4, p. 89

A recipe in the *Kama Sutra* states:

'*Rams' or he-goats' testicles boiled in sugared milk increase sexual prowess.*'

Homer wrote that Achilles ate the bone marrow of lions for courage and strength, and the Hindu physician Susrata (1400 B.C.) is said to have prescribed the eating of genital glands of young tigers to cure impotence. Ancient advice to people to eat glands (which had the effect of supplying them with hormones) is perhaps the precursor to the modern science of endocrinology, the study of glands.

Heart heals heart, kidneys heal kidneys, similia similibus curantur. – Paracelsus

Whatever the primary aim, the underlying desire to enhance sensual pleasure was never far from the medical or culinary search for aphrodisiacs.

Gender Specifics

Phallo-centric societies where the succession of a male heir is paramount are, not surprisingly, obsessed with potency and virility. In her book

Aphrodite, Isabelle Allende notes that this is understandable given 'the limitations of the capricious *male appendage that is wont to fade from the surfeit, if not from the owner's shortcomings'*.

Member Enhancements

Among the many recipes found in Shaykh Nefzawi's Arabian manual of love *The Perfumed Garden* is the usefully entitled 'A prescription for increasing the dimensions of small members and for making them splendid.'

This appears to be a universal issue and in the following recipe written by Tun Hsuan Tzu in the *Art of the Bedchamber* (a book that hails from the time of the Chinese Ming Dynasty), an extra three inches is guaranteed!

The (vital) Ingredients

3 fen (.36 grams) of top quality *jou ch'ung Jung* (a Chinese herb)

2 fen of hai *tsoa,* a type of seaweed ground into powder.

So far so easy but then the instructions continue:

'Find a white dog born in the first moon of the year. Use the secretion of its liver to mix the powder into a form of paste, then apply to your jade stem (penis) three times. At dawn, the following day draw some fresh water from the well and wash it off. *Your jade stem will definitely grow three inches longer.*' [43]

Upright Members

All the earliest aphrodisiacal sources, from the *Kama Sutra, The Ananga Ranga*, and *The Perfumed Garden*, to the culinary books of Ancient Rome and Greece, contain advice and recipes to guard against male erectile dysfunction.

Indeed, such is the need, the most poisonous, vile, revolting and foul foodstuffs have been tried. There seem to be no lengths to which man will not go in order to remain potent.

Pink Pleasure

Women, on the other hand, were historically more concerned with aphrodisiac assistance to fecundity than to libido. Women also used them as enticements to keep their males from wandering.

The humble gingerbread man was originally baked by lovelorn women to resemble their

---

43 Hendrickson, Robert *Lewd Food: The Complete Guide to Aphrodisiac Edibles* Chilton Book Company, 1974, p. 275

heart's desire. Once eaten by the man in question, his heart and loins would be in thrall to the damsel ever after.

Sweet Teeth

Other aphrodisiacs were traditionally served to cleanse the mouth, or used as aromatic astringents particularly in times before dental hygiene, when most mouths were repellent orifices.

Contrary and Practical Aphrodisiacs

An alternative but effective method for those less able in the kitchen is to provoke temptation by fasting and abstinence. Isabelle Allende cites a tradition from the Middle Ages where before the wedding, bride and groom would sleep naked in a bed for three nights without touching to heighten their desire.

Anti-Aphrodisiacs

To quell one's ardour, should the problem ever arise, John Davenport, author of *Aphrodisiacs and Anti-Aphrodisiacs*, recommended the study of mathematics. 'In all ages, mathematicians have been but little disposed to love.' Then again one could try walking barefoot, a method advised by both Plato and Aristole.

— Inside Love's Larder —

At some time or other all foods have been classified as potentially... potent. As 19th century writer John Davenport put it: 'The vegetable, animal, and mineral kingdoms have been ransacked for the purpose of discovering remedies capable for strengthening the genital apparatus, and exciting it to action.' [44]

That said, there are essentials no self-respecting '*connoisseur of seduction*' or '*gastronome of love*' would go without. These I have termed the basic **Ingredients of Love** followed by a list of **Forbidden Fruits** and **Venerous Vegetables**. Lastly, for those with a taste for the more exotic, there is a selection of **Fetishistic Food...**

So, dear Reader, when you are quite ready...

---

44 Davenport, John *Aphrodisiacs and Anti-aphrodisiacs: Three Essays on the Powers of Reproduction* London: privately printed, 1869. [EBook #27752]

...Will you walk into my parlour said the spider to the fly...

Dear friend, what shall I do?
To prove the warm affection
I have always felt for you.
I have within my pantry
Good store of all that's nice;
I'm sure you're very welcome –
Will you please to take a slice.
'Oh, no, no!' said the little fly,
'Kind sir, that cannot be;
I've heard what's in your pantry,
And I do not wish to see.
– Mary Howitt

— Ingredients Of Love —

Fish

Apuleuis, 2nd c. author of *The Golden Ass*, wrote that love potions composed mainly of shellfish, 'must necessarily have great efficacy in exciting women to venery in as much as Venus herself was born of the sea.' Evolutionists would surely concur, for did we not ourselves emerge from the watery depths?

Fish may be cold-blooded creatures by nature, but they are also prolific and by analogy, symbolize fecundity. Nutritionally high in phosphorous and iodine, they contain vitamins A and D, deemed aphrodisiacal.

Dr Jacobus X, author of *Genital Laws*, claimed that eating fish could activate spermatic secretions[45], something reinforced by many ancient cults, who forbade their celibate priests to eat seafood.

Greek poet Asclepiad strongly advocated a meal consisting of 'three large fish, ten smaller

---

45 Hendrickson, Robert *Lewd Food: The Complete Guide to Aphrodisiac Edibles* Chilton Book Company, 1974, p. 18

ones and twenty-four shrimp for anyone planning an evening with a willing woman.' In Hebrew, the word "nun" has the duel meaning of *fish* and *vagina*. Rabelais extolled fish as the food of harlots. Citing Strobo and Pliny, he wrote that the waters of the Nile were 'so prolific that Egyptian women brought forth their brats four at a time.'

'We have observed,' wrote Dr. Nicolas Venette in his 17th century book *Tableau d'Amour Conjugal* 'that those who live almost entirely on shellfish and fish are more ardent in love than all others.'

Catch of the Day

For guaranteed potency, Marcus Gavius Apicius, the Roman gourmet and lover of refined luxury, swore by tuna, red mullet, sea bream and squid, but the following list shows there is an abundance of choice.

Fishy Aphrodisiacs

Abalone

Anchovies

Barbell

Bouillabaisse (a French fish stew originating from Marseilles)

Boutargue (a paste prepared from dried and mashed grey mullet, believed to increase the output of seminal fluid; popular as an hors d'oeuvre in the sensuous salons of 18th c. France)

Carp

Caviar

Clams

Cockles

Cod (Rabelais devotes ten pages to the cod albeit as a euphemism for what lies under the codpiece)

Cod Liver Oil

Cod Roe

Crab

Crayfish

Cuttlefish

Eels

Fish Soups

Frogs Legs

Haddock

Halibut

Herring

Herring Roe

Kipper

Lampreys ('one of my passions,' declared Queen Elizabeth 1st, although Henry I and King John are both said to have died from over indulgence thereof, as did Charles V of Spain.)

Lobster

Mackerel

Mullet

Mussels

Octopus

Perch

Pike

Plaice

Salmon (it goes through so much to spawn that it is deemed an aphriodisiac. Indeed the 19th century American cookbook 'How to Keep a Husband,' recommends trying 'salmon en papilotte' or simply fried in butter with salt.)

Scallops
Sea Bream

Shellfish ('Shellfish are the prime cause of the decline of morals and the adaptation of an extravagant lifestyle,' according to Pliny the Elder, (A.D. 23-79).)

Shrimp (The Japanese like their ebi alive. Ebi odori is made by shelling gutting and splitting a shrimp down the middle, after which the creature's nerves still functioning, is pressed into a small ball of rice continuing to wriggle until popped into the mouth.)

Sea Fruits (what the French call seaweed and related seafood, such as Eryngoes; 'The Puritanical Ladies Dictionary' of 1649 warned their readers, 'Eryngoes are not good to be taken & lust provoking meats must be forsaken.')

Sea Urchins (emit the intense odour of the oceans deep and erotic. 'The taste is pure iodine and salt to the non-initiate, for the cognoscenti it makes a mouthful as we say worthy of a cardinal.'[46])

Snails (Roman author Petronius recommended a breed of snails fattened on milk until they became too plump to crawl back into their shells.)

Snakes

Sturgeon

Squid

Tripe

Trout

Tuna

Turbot

Turbut Roe

Turtle

Whiting

And saving the best (or most effective) until last...

---

46 Allende, Isabel *Aphrodite, A Memoir of the Senses* Flamingo 1998, p. 140

Oysters

Oysters are more beautiful than any religion...
There's nothing in Christianity or Buddhism that quite
matches the sympathetic unselfishness of an oyster.
– Saki (Hector Hugh Munro) Scottish writer
(1870-1916)

Known as the 'vulva fish' by the Danes, the oyster is held both from medical and psychological standpoints in the highest esteem by lovers the world over. Eric Partridge's *'Dictionary of Slang and Unconventional English'* gives one definition of the oyster as 'the female pudenda, they arouse our libidinal thoughts, men are stimulated by bivalves's mucous consistency.'

Nutritionally, the oyster is high in iron and zinc, which raises sperm and testosterone production and increases the libido. Oysters contain omega-3 fatty acids, considered to increase one's overall wellbeing and even fight depression. An exceptionally easy food to digest, they each contain only 7 calories. Seneca rhapsodized *'beneficent Oyster exciting rather than sating, all stomachs digest you, all stomachs bless you.'*

Most people prefer oysters, as the French do, 'like a girl at her best with the fewest possible clothes and the less make-up the better.' Pauline Bonaparte, sister of Napoleon, is said to have bathed daily in milk whilst being fed fresh oysters and champagne by her favourite slave. Apparently, she had acquired a taste for black men whilst living in Santo Domingo and when forced to return to France, took one with her. Lord Byron decreed they were indeed amatory food, and Casanova declared that 'so delicate a morsel must be a sin in itself,' famously starting his day with fifty of these marvelous mollusks.

Oyster's Kisses – Shared Tongue to Tongue
This, a favourite love game of Casanova's, invariably led, or so he tells us, to the *piece de résistance*. He practised it with lovers Armelline and Emilie and wrote *'we then sucked the oysters in, one by one after placing them on the other's lips. Voluptuous readers try it and kill me whether it is not the nectar of the gods!'*

A more daring version involved Casanova letting the oyster slip not on his lover's lips but between her ample bosom and lower still...

Should you ever find yourself in such a situation but have trouble opening the oyster, Dr H. F. Prytherch of the US Fish and Wildlife Service[47] advises dipping the oysters in carbonated water, which makes them relax and let go of their shells.

Caviar

Caviar is to dining what a sable coat is to a girl in evening dress.' – Ludwig Bemelmans, author and gourmet

Our appreciation of these bubble bursts of sensuous saltiness is measured by their rarity, exclusivity and price. These pearls of the Caspian Sea are salted sturgeon eggs (red caviar are salmon eggs). Caviar is the perfect aphrodisiac, super high in zinc, vitamin A and Omega-3 fatty acids. It helps to increase blood flow, stimulate testosterone production and promote sperm development. The largest eggs, called *beluga* are the most expensive and come from the largest fish. The highest-grade beluga is a pale to dark grey in colour. *Osietra* are medium sized eggs containing about 50 per gram and grey to golden brown

47 Hendrickson, Robert *Lewd Food: The Complete Guide to Aphrodisiac Edibles* Chilton Book Company, 1974, p. 58

in colour. Lastly, *sevruga*, the smallest eggs have about 70 per gram and are dark grey to black.

Appropriately enough the word Caviar comes from 'khav-yar,' the Persian word meaning 'cake of strength'.

References to caviar in literature and art date back as far as the sturgeon itself. According to some of the more esoteric writings of Aristotle, lavish Greek banquets usually ended with a brass horn section announcing the arrival of heaped platters of caviar, garnished with flowers. The Persians believed caviar could aid a multitude of illnesses, and would eat it in stick form to give them energy and stamina. Medieval English society held the caviar-producing sturgeon in the greatest respect. King Edward II proclaimed the sturgeon to be a 'royal fish' and decreed that all sturgeon caught in England belonged to the imperial treasury and must be given to the monarch or the gentry. In fact, by the Middle Ages many European countries' sovereigns had claimed rights to the sturgeon.

As the main consumers of caviar in Russia, the czars levied a caviar tax on sturgeon fishermen. Nicholas II was given 11 tons of the finest caviar annually by his fisherman subjects and especially enjoyed the caviar of the sterlet sturgeon, with its small golden eggs. It proved so popular with Russian nobility that this species is all but extinct today.

Many American states also produced caviar. Sold at a penny a pound, American caviar was served in saloons like modern day beer-nuts. It was hoped that the saltiness of the dish would make bar patrons thirstier and bigger spenders on beer. Some patrons even put caviar in their beer, creating what was called 'Albany beer.'[48]

Over-fishing led to the collapse of the US caviar industry. During the caviar boom at the end of the nineteenth century, much of the American caviar exported to Europe was then fraudulently re-imported as Russian Caviar, as many thought it superior-tasting to the home harvested caviar.

Under cover of the clinking of water goblets and silverware and bone china, I paved my plate with chicken slices. Then I covered the chicken slices with caviar thickly as if I were spreading peanut butter on a piece of bread. Then I picked up the chicken slices in my fingers one by one,

---

48 Meredith B. Gordon *Such Stuff as Dreams are Made On: The Story of Caviar, from Prehistory to the Present* http://leda.law.harvard.edu/leda/data/504/Gordon.html#fn20

rolled them so the caviar wouldn't ooze off and ate them.
– Sylvia Plath, American poet (1932-1963)

Geoduck Clam
An enormous inter-tidal clam, it shamelessly exposes its huge neck as it suns itself. Considered visually offensive, ladies of an earlier day were advised to stay at a discreet distance. [49]

Turtle
This most aristocratic seafood is the only food 'hung for our sins to come'. The turtle's extended head and neck resembles the male member and when exposed is lassoed and then hung up, after which it takes an arsenal of tools to extract it from its shell. It is said to make an excellent 'love soup.'

Eel
Slippery fare, the obviously phallic eel has always been held in esteem and enjoyed in the top echelons of society.

The ancient Greeks served eels with oysters and roasted grasshoppers, whilst Roman epicureans delighted in all varieties of the eel. The

---

49 Hendrickson, Robert *Lewd Food: The Complete Guide to Aphrodisiac Edibles* Chilton Book Company, 1974, p. 37

child emperor Heliogalabus kept a large fishing fleet solely to catch eels for their roe and it is recorded that Romans fed their congers on unfortunate Christian slaves.

The ancient Letts, a people famed for their love songs, called the male sex organs 'an eel's head and small onions' and the vagina 'an eel pot or eel river'.

A most erotic recipe 'Ye Collar Eeles' is found in the *Lucayos Cook Book* (1660), which recommends that in preparation, both lovers 'take your eeles and rub them with salt till all the skinnes is quite taken off'.

Brillat-Savarin recounts a tale of a three-foot eel fed to friars by a certain Madame Briguet. The presentation of the eel was so suggestive that the conversation 'settled on the most popular of mortal sins and remained there.'

The Lobster

Oh have ye heard of monger Meg,
And how she loved the weaver, O
She let me see her red-haired coynte,
And sold it for a lobster, O...
– Robert Burns, *Merry Muses*

A firm favourite of all proverbial lotharios, this kingly crustacean has been enjoyed since prehistoric times, as evidenced by excavations revealing shell heaps and kitchen middens at least 10,000 years old. Fished commercially from 1800, the lobster like the oyster has, over time, metamorphosed from food deemed fit only for the poor to fare of the affluent. It has been recorded that the King of London, a famous 19th century pimp, regaled his girls with huge lobsters as well as plump oysters and pieces of crawfish (small lobsters without claws).

The bawdy film adaptation of Henry Fielding's classic 18th century novel, Tom Jones, features one of the most memorable depictions of human sexual appetite. The scene in question is between playboy Tom and, (unknowingly) possibly his mother, Mrs Waters. Facing each other, the table laden with large steaming pewter bowls of soup, the teasing Mrs Waters lustily slurps big round spoonfuls, breasts tumbling out of her bodice. So begins the feast. Tom rips a claw off the langoustine he is holding and greedily sucks on it. Mrs Waters mimics his gesture turning her face to profile. The pair, whose lips glisten with gravy, suck, slurp and joyously consume the spread of ale, turkey, oysters, pears, and wine. And then each other.

— Sins Of The Flesh —

If a man will passionately give himself up to the enjoyment of coition without undergoing great fatigue he must live upon strengthening foods... the quality of the sperm depends directly on the food you take.

— The Perfumed Garden

Meat has been held in high regard by practically every ancient sex manual, bar, of course, those of the vegetarian Hindus. High in protein, the bloodthirsty early nomadic Tartars liked their meat raw. Indeed, to this day steak *tartare* is enjoyed as potent fare.

Philip Roth's famous hero Portnoy also has a penchant for raw meat, although his desire bypasses his digestive system. Portnoy masturbates with the raw liver his mother had planned on using for dinner.

Beefsteak, being a common term for a well-made young man, is as a viande equally well-liked. Posh cuts include filet mignon, Chateaubriand, Tournedos, Beef Wellington and the aristocrat of steak, 'Sir loin'.

It is said that either King Henry VIII, James I

or Charles II (who have all been cited in the telling of the story) was so pleased with a succulent slice of pink meat that he unsheathed his sword, laid it on the brown crested sirloin and knighted it.[50]

However, in the epicurean stakes, its place has been usurped by the ever-so-privileged, hand-massaged and beer drinking Japanese Kobe beef (Wadakin, or Matsuzaka) from Mt. Fugi.

Well-Hung Meat

In 1300 B.C. Chinese playboy King Chou–hsin built an artificial lake and landscaped the woods near his palace. He then filled the lake with wine and hung meat from the trees. Assigning 300 warriors to swagger about this earthly paradise for his voyeuristic entertainment, he encouraged them to eat and drink at will, and then forced these warriors to ravish maidens, who were let loose daily. [51]

---

50 'It is, perhaps, a pity to spoil so noble a story; but the interests of truth demand that we declare that sirloin is probably a corruption of surloin, which signifies the upper part of a loin, the prefix sur being equivalent to over or above. In French we find this joint called surlonge, which so closely resembles our sirloin, that we may safely refer the two words to a common origin. Mrs. Beeton, Isabella The Book of Household Management First Published in a Bound Edition 1861. http://www.gutenberg.org/cache/epub/10136/pg10136.html
51 Hendrickson, Robert Lewd Food: The Complete Guide to Aphrodisiac Edibles Chilton Book Company, 1974, p. 139

On the wild side

Most wild animal meats are what nutritionists call 'analeptic' or strength-giving. Artemis, the Greek Goddess of Wildlife, was also a fertility goddess and our word 'venery' (the pursuit or indulgence in sexual pleasure) derives from the French *vineries* referring to the art of hunting.

Wild meat is rich in azezome and protein. Interestingly, the liver was widely believed by the ancients to be the seat of sexual desire.

To encourage my jaded body I applied to myself strong meats... so great was my care to acquit myself honourably with my mistress. – Petronius

Rabbit

Rabbit has long been associated with sexual strength and license. Eating the foetus of a hare was said to end barrenness forever. Pliny asserted that if a pregnant woman ate the testicles, womb or rennet of a hare, she would always bear virile boys. Richard II and Henry VIII were said to be very fond of Coynes (rabbits) and author Alexander Dumas recommended Rabbit tongues. A simple dish to make: allow ten tongues per person, scald the tongue, cool and skin.

Swamp Rabbit Milk

In the early 1900s, Silent George of Shawnee-town increased the joy of sex in Illinois by selling canned Swamp Rabbit Milk. It was thus named to conjure up mental images of the legendary mating habit of rabbits. Golden spray-painted cans of condensed milk were re-labeled by the ingenious George declaring the contents to be rich in vitamins J, U, M and P. The milk was described as a balanced formula for unbalanced people. [52]

Bear Meat

Bear meat was said by the ancients to bestow courage, youth and strength, enabling a man to bear hug his lover until she yields. Bear paw is a Chinese favourite and the Chinese philosopher Mencuis described it as being 'so smooth and delicious it melts in your mouth'.

Venison (including deer, moose, elk and caribou)

King Solomon fed his 700 wives and 300 concubines great quantities of harts (stags), roebucks

---

[52] http://www.ncbi.nlm.nih.gov/pmc/articles/PMC1862207/pdf/canmedajo1378-0124c.pdf

JH Young "Nutritional eccentricities". Human Nutrition. Current Issues and Controversies. Edited by A. Neuberger and T.H. Jukes. Englewood, NJ, 1982 and deer. The Romans liked deer grilled at their orgies and Holy Roman Emperor Charlemagne, a father of fifty, often breakfasted on a whole joint of venison. In *Don Quixote*, Cervantes writes of venison hanging off tree branches for the marriage feast of Camacho the Rich. Deer horns ground into a powder and added to love tonics are still popular in Russia.

A classic English dish is of 'umbles'; the heart, liver and entrails of deer. A perquisite of the huntsmen, 'umbles' were traditionally made into a pie – hence the phrase eating humble pie.

Blooming Albumen

'I have taken nothing to-day but a cup of chocolate and a salad of whites of eggs dressed with oil from Lucca and Marseilles vinegar.'

'But, dearest, it is folly! You must be ill?'

'Yes, I am just now, but I shall be all right when I have distilled the whites of eggs, one by one, into your amorous soul.'

'I did not think you required any such stimulants.'

'Who could want any with you? But I have a rational fear, for if I happened to prime without being able to fire, I would blow my brains out.'[53]

---

53 Casanova wrote in his memoirs CHAPTER XVIII Vol II from *Paris to Prison*.

Casanova in conversation with M. M. (Marie-Mathtilde) at the Casino of Muran In the presence of her lover *The Complete Memoirs* CHAPTER XVIII Vol 11 from *Paris to Prison*.

Eggs

The egg is one of our most ancient fertility symbols. Consumed raw before engaging in sex they enhance one's libido, a belief exquisitely evoked in the Japanese film *Tampopo* directed by Itami. The film features a highly erotic scene were the two protagonists pass a raw egg yolk from mouth to mouth until finally it oozes from the actress's lips as she comes to a climatic shudder. The *Lucayos Cookbook* (1660) claimed that for aphrodisiac purposes, duck eggs were superior to hen's and pigeon's eggs superior to duck's. The sparrow, it decreed, gave the greatest egg of all.

Greek god of love, Eros, is said to have hatched from an egg. It was traditional for Persian brides on their wedding nights to hurl eggs against the bedroom door and in so doing, hoped their own maidenhead would break as quickly. People of the Congo believed that a lady who ate any kind of egg was open to all and any male overtures.

The Chinese regard the egg as the ideal love food because it contains the negative and positive, the Yin and Yang, the yolk representing the sun and the white, the moon.

He who will feed for several days on eggs cooked with myrrh, cinnamon and pepper will find an increased vigour in his erection and his capacity for coition. His member shall be in such a turgid state that it will seem as if it could never return to a state of repose.
— *The Perfumed Garden*

Fowl Play
'Sparrow baked and given to a woman in her drink,' Cyranus wrote *'will make her dissolve and melt away for love'*.

Birds valued for their supposed aphrodisiac qualities (evinced in their extremely amorous disposition) include sparrows, pigeons, turtledoves and partridges.

In 1999, France outlawed the eating of the endangered Ortolan, a tiny songbird no bigger than a thumb. This epicurean delicacy is captured (unharmed) and left in a dark box, where the lack of light prompts it to gorge itself. Then, when plumped up to three or four times its normal size, the bird is drowned in a snifter of armangac, quickly roasted for six or eight minutes and served hot.

To eat it the diner covers his head beneath a white napkin. The suggested reasons for this are twofold, either to hide his shame from God on eating such a creature or to capture the rising aromas. The head is snapped off and the remainder, bones and all, is eaten. Most famously, the ortolan appeared on the menu of former French President François Mitterand's last meal in 1998. A week before dying of cancer, Mitterrand ordered a grand feast for 30 that included oysters, foie gras and a long row of two-ounce ortolans. By some accounts, Mitterrand polished off two.[54]

Pate Patois
Goosy, Goosy Gander
Where do you wander?
Up town down town
In my ladies chamber....

Foie Gras
One of the most luxurious foods is foie gras.

[54] http://today.msnbc.msn.com/id/9687163

With its buttery texture and mythical status, it is expensive, decadent and sought the world over.

Ancient Egyptians, Greeks and Romans all favoured the exquisite taste of the fattened goose liver. In Roman times, geese were crammed with figs and Cato, Columella and Palladius all give instructions for making the delicacy. Emperor Heliogabalus, noted for his brief reign (A.D. 218-222) of debauched excesses, fed foie gras to his dogs.

As with preparing the ortolan, the preparation of foie gras is a cruel process. Each goose is tied down – only the neck can move – and it is force-fed by 'goose fatteners' or 'crammers' six times a day using their middle fingers to push down a paste of maize, chestnut flour and buck wheat flour – hence the saying 'I am stuffed as a goose.'

The most famous brands come from Strasbourg and Parizeau, in the Perigord region of France.

The ideal accompaniment to foie gras is usually a Sauterne or sherry, though there are some who advocate Madeira port or even champagne. Grimod de la Reyniere drank Swiss absinthe with foie gras. Nothing, he declared, surpasses an excellent pate de foie gras. 'They have killed more gourmands than the plague'.

To 'goose' is to poke or pinch between the buttocks and in French the le petite oie refers to the female pudendum.

Avisodomy is a sadistic and perverted sexual practise, mentioned in the memoirs of both the Marquis de Sade and founder of Hustler magazine Larry Flynt. Performed with live geese, the goose is literally... goosed... whilst its neck is twisted and then wrung off at the point of ejaculation. This ensures the "pleasurable" benefit of the spasming of the anal sphincter in the dying animal. Adding insult to injury the goose is then plucked and eaten.

Black and White Truffles

Let's drink the health of truffles black
In gratitude we must not lack
For they assure us dominance
In all erotic alliance
As an aid to lovers' bliss
Fate pleasurably fashioned this
Rarity divine gods send

To use forever without end. [55]

'Presently, we were aware of an odour gradually coming towards us, something musky, fiery, savoury, mysterious, – a hot drowsy smell, that lulls the senses, and yet enflames them, – the truffles were coming.' – William Makepeace Thackeray (1811-1863), a famous gourmand and writer who loved food so much he died from overeating.

For centuries, truffles known as the *black diamonds of the table*, and the gastronome's *sancta sanctorum*, have been considered by the illustrious as the ultimate aphrodisiac.

Archaeologists excavating a 4000 year-old Amorite palace in what is now eastern Syria found remnants of truffles in special baskets and listed in the palace's inventory. Cicero called them 'the daughters of the Earth conceived by the Sun.' The poet Juvenal urged the Libyans to 'keep your wheat and send us your truffles.' The Romans dedicated the fungus to Venus in the correct belief that it stimulated love.

Early Greeks and Romans believed that the truffle sprang from the earth spawned from the seminal fluid of mating deer. In the Middle

55 Hendrickson, Robert *Lewd Food: The Complete Guide to Aphrodisiac Edibles* Chilton Book Company, 1974, p. 166

Ages people thought the white varieties sprouted from witches' spit. The most esteemed of truffles are the Italian white truffles (*tartufi bianchi*) found in the province of Alba. The cultivation of truffles is still a mystery. French peasant Joseph Talon discovered the first indirect cultivation in the 19th century. He planted acorns from truffle-growing areas and was surprised to be able to harvest truffles under young trees a few years afterwards.

Gastronome Brillat-Savarin noted that 'truffles are conducive to erotic pleasure' and scientific research has since shown that the fungus produces a steroid identical to a pheromone produced by boars during pre-mating behavior, which is also secreted by humans, but in much lower concentrations than in pigs.

Napoleon ate truffles before his trysts with Josephine. Rasputin prescribed them to thicken the Tsar's blood and strengthen the royal bloodline and George Sand called them *la pomme féérique* or fairy-like apples.

Chocolate

If any man has drunk a little too deeply from the cup of physical pleasure; if he has spent too much time at his desk that should have been spent asleep; if his fine spirits have become temporarily dulled; if he finds the air too damp, the minutes too slow, and the atmosphere too heavy to withstand; if he is obsessed by a fixed idea which bars him from any freedom of thought: if he is any of these poor creatures, we say, let him be given a good pint of amber-flavored chocolate... and marvels will be performed.

– Jean-Anthelme Brillat-Savarin (1755-1826)

Chocolate, the ultimate taste of sweet surrender, is made from beans taken from the cacoa pod of the evergreen tree, *Theobroma cacoa*. Chocolate contains theobromine, a stimulating alkaloid similar to caffeine, which helps the brain produce serotonin. The Ecuadorians called them *pepe de oro*; 'seeds of gold' and the beans were used as currency by both the Aztecs and Mayans.

Bishop de Landa who ministered to Cortez' soldiers, noted that 'he who wants a Mayan public woman for his lustful use can have one for eight to ten cacao beans.'

The first beans to reach Europe were brought back by Columbus but they were largely ignored until Cortez brought chocolate to Spain in 1527. He explained that Montezuma imbibed this drink before entering his harem, a fact seized upon by the French clergy.[56]

...The damnable agent of necromancers and sorcerers. It is well to abstain from chocolate in order to avoid the familiarity and company of a nation so suspected of sorcery (Spain).
– French cleric (1620)

Denounced as the inflamer of immorality, the Spanish kept chocolate to themselves, but by 1657 the elicit drink had become very popular in France and had even crossed the channel to set up home in the English Chocolate House (or chocolate cafes.)

Tea my learned friend... inspires scandal and sentiment; coffee excites the imagination, but chocolate sir is an aphrodisiac.[57]
– Dr Bushwhacker

Royal Hot Chocolate
(Louis XV's favourite drink)
Louis XIV popularised the consumption of chocolate at the Court of Versailles; however, Louis XV was considered the greatest lover of the cocoa-based drink.

---

56 Hendrickson, Robert *Lewd Food: The Complete Guide to Aphrodisiac Edibles* Chilton Book Company, 1974, p. 317
57 From *The Sayings of Dr Bushwhacker and Other Learned Men* (1867) by Cozzens Frederick S published by New York, A Simpson & Co

'Place the same quantity of chocolate bars and glasses of water in a coffee maker and boil gently; when you are ready to serve, place one egg yolk for four servings and stir over a gentle heat but do not boil.'[58]

In 1770, when Marie-Antoinette married Louis XVI, she arrived at the Court of Versailles with her own chocolate maker, who was given the very official title of 'Chocolate Maker to the Queen'. The chocolate maker invented new recipes and mixed the chocolate with orange blossom and sweet almonds. However, cocoa beans only became accessible to the public in the 19th century with the arrival of major factories with such famous names as the English Cadbury's and French Menier.

Honey

> Thy lips, O my spouse deep as the honeycomb honey and milk are under thy tongue, and the smell of your garments is like the smell of Lebanon.
>
> — The Song of Solomon 4:11

---

58 Court dinners or the Art of working different foods for the best restaurants based on the four seasons, by Menon, 1755 (BN, V.26995, volume IV, p. 331)

A universal love food, honey was often described as a divine substance that fell from heaven. The Arabs believed that eating honey prolonged the sexual act. In Roman mythology, Cupid, the god of love, dipped his arrows in honey before smiting lovers, while the Chinese utilized it as a binder in aphrodisiac drinks. One love potion that was popular among the Byzantines was a cake made with donkey milk and honey.

An Eastern European custom persists whereby a spoonful of honey is poured into the palms of newly married couples. They must lick it off each other as a sign that they will now take all their food together and to ensure the husband will not lift his hand to his wife except to caress her, and none but loving words will spring to the wife's lips.[59]

Attila the Hun believed steadfastly in its stimulating power. He drank so much mead (wine mixed with honey) on the day of this wedding that he died of cardiac arrest, much to the jubilation of his enemies and possibly even his bride.

---

59 Ekdah, Raviez Marilyn, *Erotic Cuisine, A Natural History of Aphrodisiac Cookery* Xlibrus Corporation, 2000, p. 165

Honey comes out of the air... At early dawn, the leaves of trees are found bedewed with honey... Whether this is the perspiration of the sky or a sort of saliva of the stars, or the moisture of the air purging itself, nevertheless it brings with it the great pleasure of its heavenly nature. It is always of the best quality when it is stored in the best flowers.

– Pliny (A.D. 23-79), Natural History, Book 20

Bread – A bun in the oven

Bread is heavy with symbolism and sensuality. Dough feels like warm living flesh and in a hot oven it swells like a rounded pregnant belly. Since the earliest of ages, bread has been baked, shaped as genitals, and anointed with body secretions. Even today, we have the phallic French baguette, which the author Isabel Allende cheekily notes: 'It is not phallic in temperament, since it is modest, trustworthy and never failing.'

In Chile, the most popular bread is called marraqueta and is shaped like the vulva. With respect to bodily secretions baked into bread, recently artist Toi Sennhauser's exhibition 'Mama's Natural Breakfast' at the Seattle Erotic Art Festival 2005 offered homemade bread, whose yeast starter included a touch of her own vaginal yeast, replacing the bread's vital force with the power of femininity.

'This is for the angel,' grandma used to say, tearing off a strip of dough for me to take into the yard. 'The angel comes to kiss it, that's all, otherwise my bread won't rise.' Sure enough, I often saw the birds come down to peck at our strip of dough. Sure enough, my grandma's bread would nearly always rise. However, I never saw an angel on the windowsill. Not even once.[60]

Rice
Another symbol of fertility, few know that throwing rice at the bride and groom as they leave the church represents the ejaculation of semen.

Milk
The first liquid to wet our lips, milk is worshiped as a liquid life force and cosmic nourishment. In the ancient world the heavens metaphorically sparkled with divine milk: both the galaxy and Milky Way were derived from the Greek word 'gala' or 'milk'.

Milk and dairy products were historically lauded for their rejuvenating and life extending properties. Paradise was frequently described as a place where honey dripped from trees and milk pails overflowed.

---

60 Jim Crace's *The Devil's Larder*; Penguin; New Ed edition (4 July 2002, p. 3-4

All but one of the *Kama Sutra's* aphrodisiac recipes contains sugar, milk, honey or clarified butter. In perhaps the most evocative sacred, erotic allegorical imagery, the Hindu God Krishna (who was raised amongst a community of cowherds and milkmaids) dances with maidens under a full moon manifesting himself as an individual lover for each woman and making love to her all night in exactly the manner she desired.[61]

---

61 Hospodar, Miriam *Aphrodisiac Foods, Bringing Heaven to Earth* Gastronomica, the Journal of Food and Culture Vol.4, p. 84

— Forbidden Fruits —

*I always determined the sexual capabilities of a woman by
the way she eats fruit. When testing a potential bed-mate
I offer her an apple or a pear to see how she eats it. Small
mincing bites – the lady-like kind – they are not good. But
if she crunches the fruit, salivates with pleasure, and crinkles
her nose in enjoyment, this girl, my friend should prove to be
a redoubtable love partner.* – Italian grand seducer and
poet Gabriele D'Annunzio.[62]

Apples

Since time immemorial, lovers have exchanged
apples as tokens of affection. When Adam suc-
cumbed to his temptress Eve and bit into the
forbidden 'apple', a lump stuck in his throat.
All men since have (at least symbolically), inher-
ited the mark of Adam's fall. However, at that
time, many different fruits were labelled apples;
pomegranates were *apples of Carthage*, tomatoes
and aubergine were *love apples*, dates were *finger
apples*, and potatoes were *apples of the earth*. It was
in fact relatively late (the 4th c.) when St Jerome
claimed the fruit at the heart of man's fall was an
apple, as we would recognize it. It is believed by

62 Hendrickson, Robert *Lewd Food: The Complete Guide to Aphrodisiac Edibles* Chilton Book
Company, 1974, p. 230

many to have actually been an apricot or a pomegranate. It is said some Muslims believe it to be a banana.

> Art thou the topmost apple?
> The gatherers could not reach
> Reddening on the bough
> Shall not I take thee
> Sappho (LIII a verse written for the apple of her eye)

It is surmised that the apple may have been chosen as the forbidden fruit because when cut in half its seeds appear arranged in the shape of the vulva.[63] 'This apple dear sisters,' warned the *Ancrene Riwle*, a 12th century manual for nuns, 'is a token of everything that arouses lust and sensual delights.' Rabelais referred to breasts as *pommes d'amour* (apples of love) and testicles as *pommes des cas pendre* (hanging apple cases).

Apricots

Known as 'sun eggs' by the ancient Greeks and Persians, apricots were also a favourite aphrodisiac at the Court of James I of England[64]. In Shakespeare's *A Midsummer Nights Dream* (Act 3

63 Allende, Isabel *Aphrodite, A Memoir of the Senses* Flamingo 1998, p. 152
64 Hendrickson, Robert *Lewd Food: The Complete Guide to Aphrodisiac Edibles* Chilton Book Company, 1974, p. 236

Scene 1), the bewitched Tatiana awakens and instructs her fairies to indulge her new found true-love Bottom.

> Be kind and courteous to this gentleman;
> Hop in his walks and gambol in his eyes;
> Feed him with apricocks and dewberries,
> With purple grapes, green figs, and mulberries;...

It should be noted though that apricot kernels contain a chemical called amygdalin, which the body can convert to cyanide. Apple, cherry and peach pips can be equally dangerous. [65]

Bananas

The banana is considered a love food because of its erotic appearance, and in many languages is a synonym for the male appendage. Loaded with potassium, magnesium and B vitamins the banana also contains chelating minerals and the bromelain enzyme, said to enhance the male libido. Central Americans drink the sap of the red banana as an aphrodisiac.

---

65 Ibid., p. 258

Cherries

The cherry is commonly used as fruity innuendo to denote virginity in pubescent young girls.

Popped Cherry Soufflé

¾ cup Cherry purée

1 tb Fresh lemon juice

3 Egg whites

1 Pinch of salt

Sugar to taste

Pit and purée enough sour cherries to make 3/4 cup. Preheat the oven to 375f. Oil a quart soufflé dish and sprinkle it with sugar. Heat the cherry purée in a small pan. Add the lemon juice, salt, and sugar to taste, and stir to blend; remove from the heat. Beat the egg whites until stiff but not dry and stir them into the hot purée until evenly blended. Spoon into the soufflé dish and bake for 20-25 minutes. Sprinkle with sherbet when cooked.[66]

Dates

Deliciously rich in both calories and vitamins, this is a high-energy food. A mere handful of these lush soft fruits are equivalent to an entire

---

66 *The Fannie Farmer Cookbook*, Alfred A. Knopf, Inc. (c) 1979.

meal. A favorite of the harems, where its dimpled flesh and rotund curves were appropriately valued, the date is said to increase potency in men and coquetry in women. The fermented juice from the crown of the date palm is used to make aphrodisiac liquor called palm wine.

Figs

> The fig tree putteth forth her green figs and the wines with the tender grape give a good smell, Arise my love my fair one and come away.
> — The Song of Songs, Book of the Old Testament

A favourite of Cleopatra's, the fig is a most sensuous fruit, soft to the touch and a visual delight. Opened, it further arouses by resembling the female sex organs. It is steeped in history: Adam and Eve wore fig leaves to hide their shame, the Romans believed it a gift of the gods, Bacchus held it sacred, and it was served at Dionysian orgies. Buddhism was born under a fig tree: the Hindus regard the fruit as resembling both the male and female genitalia. To the ancient Greeks, figs were more precious than gold. Associated with fertility it was traditional in some

Southern European countries for wedding guests
to throw figs instead of rice at the bride and groom.

The poet and author D.H. Lawrence describes it thus:

Figs

The proper way to eat a fig, in society,

Is to split it in four, holding it by the stump,

And open it, so that it is a glittering, rosy, moist, honied

and heavy-petalled, four-petalled flower.

… Every fruit has its secret.

The fig is a very secretive fruit

As you see it standing, growing, you feel at once it is symbolic:

And it seems male.

But when you come to know it better, you agree with

the Romans

It is female.

The Italians vulgarly say, it stands for the female part;

The fig fruit:

The fissure, the yoni,

The wonderful moist conductivity toward the centre…

The language of the fig is scatological, used as a derogatory term for a homosexual, or to refer to female genitalia. In Turkish it means anus and for Arabs to nibble a fig is to perform cunnilingus.

It will delight the tongue if soaked in orange liquor, and served with whipped cream.

Mulberries

Fruit of the Chinese tree upon which silk worms feed, these berries are known as 'the fruit of lost youth'. There remain to this day in London some of the gnarled old trees from among a hundred thousand planted in the early 17th century by King James I.[67]

Nectarines

> *Talking of Pleasure, this moment I was writing with one hand, and with the other holding to my Mouth a Nectarine – how good how fine. It went down all pulpy, slushy, oozy, all its delicious embonpoint melted down my throat like a large, beatified Strawberry.*
>
> – John Keats (1795-1821)

---

67 Lewd Food Hendrickson, Robert *Lewd Food: The Complete Guide to Aphrodisiac Edibles* Chilton Book Company, 1974, p. 247

Peaches

Utterly peachy... usually associated with feminine beauty, the skin of the peach is reminiscent of a youthful complexion. This succulent, moist, intensely sensual fruit is highly versatile and can be dried, baked, stewed, pickled, used in love potions, even as a hair restorer (according to Nicholas Culpepper author of *The Complete Herbal*, 1652).

If the kernels be bruised and boiled in vinegar until they become thick, it marvellously makes the hair to grow again upon the bald places or where it is too thin.

In China, there is the legendary Banto peach, which requires 300 years to fully ripen and will bestow health, virility and everlasting life on those fortunate to find it.[68]

Clustered in a walled garden, nude Persian houri
bending over a well.
All pink and yellow and dimpled and juicily cleft as
Renoir's dappled Baigneauses, *oeils de boeuf d'or*.

---

68 Hendrickson, Robert *Lewd Food: The Complete Guide to Aphrodisiac Edibles* Chilton Book Company, 1974. p250

alternatively, aspiring odoriferously, they lie heaped
in pyramids as if sun warmed Aztec temples.
To eat one: cunnilingus with pubescent cherubim
And then the gardener's grandmother in the
wrinkled pit
– William Fahey [69]

The Pomegranate

This 'love fruit' of the ancient civilizations of the
Middle East is a symbol of fertility. The Romans
believed its ovules to be an aphrodisiac, a belief
that in later centuries spread to all parts of Europe.
According to Pliny the Elder, the pith of the pomegranate was conducive to sexual activity, and the
physical structure of the fruit was viewed as en-
riching and invigorating, i.e. many seeds of a rich,
brilliant red colour. The *Kama Sutra* promotes the
use of the seeds for the enlargement of the penis.

Pumpkin... Pie

In a study conducted in 1995 to discover the most
erotically stimulating aromas, pumpkin pie was
found to increase penile blood flow by 40 percent.
This surprising discovery made by neurologist
and psychiatrist Alan Hirsh at the Smell and Taste

---

69 Ekdah, Raviez Marilyn, *Erotic Cuisine, A Natural History of Aphrodisiac Cookery* Xlibrus Corporation, 2000, p. 146

Treatment and Research Foundation in Chicago, confounded sexologists and perfumers.

Quince
An apple-like fruit which the Romans considered as sacred to Venus, the quince is also regarded as a symbol of aging love.

> The lines I see upon thy face
> Surpass the bloom of youthful grace
> Thy quinces drooping in my hand
> Outshine young breasts that upright stand
> Winter than summer seems more warm
> And springtime yields to autumn's charm
> – Paulus Silentiarius

Strawberry and Raspberry
The early Greeks had a taboo against the eating of any red food including wild strawberries. Thus, the berry acquired a certain mystique in edible erotica and is often a culinary euphemism for the nipple.

Napoleon's chef, Louis de Cuss, invented Fraises *a la Cussy*: a dessert of strawberries, cream and champagne.

Rubens' Sweeties

The pear, shaped as a Rubens' nude, has been celebrated in art, song and poetry as far back as 1000 B.C. It is one of the few fruits that ripen better off the tree.

Rhubarb

Italian lovers mix rhubarb in wine with cinnamon, ginger and vanilla for a stimulating aphrodisiac tonic. However, the leaves of the rhubarb and peach are extremely poisonous.

Passion Fruit

The name says it all.

Nuts (about you)

These are nuggets rich in protein, amino acids, magnesium, iron, calcium, and phosphorus and are historically regarded as highly aphrodisiacal.

Almonds

Throughout antiquity the almond has been used to represent fertility and euphemistically, testicles. Its aroma supposedly arouses passion in women.

Alexandre Dumas dined on almond soup every night before meeting his mistress, and Samson wooed Delilah with these tasty nuts. In mythology, the almond emerges from the vulva of the goddess Cybele and is mentioned 73 times in the Old Testament.

In the 15th century Arabic sex manual *The Perfumed Garden* it is written that:

> *He who feels that he is weak for coition should drink before going to bed a glass full of very thick honey and eat twenty almonds.*

The almond is associated with beauty, virility, as a harbinger of spring and the expectancy of new life. An essential part of Arabian pastries, in Italy it is used as a medicine and tonic for the heartsick, which may be the origin of the custom of offering almonds before a meal with cocktails.

Pistachios
A small fruit very popular in all of Asia and mentioned in the Bible and in Persian and Arab writings.

That old... Chestnut

> Chestnuts are *'delicacies for princes and a lusty and masculine food for rusticks, and able to make women well-complexioned.'*
> – John Evelyn (1620-1706), English writer, gardener and diarist

Widely used in Chinese love dishes, the chestnut was also a favourite in 16th century Elizabethan England with dishes consisting of chestnuts soaked in wine and then cooked with cinnamon, pistachio nuts, pine kernels, rocket seeds and sugar.

Chestnuts, according to Dr Ivan Block in his book *Odaratus Sexualis* (1933), have the odour of semen.

Peanuts
Rich in vitamin E (the sexuality vitamin) peanuts are recommended by various sexologists.

Potent Peanut Butter Soup

Sauté ½ a cup of finely chopped onion in one table-spoon of vegetable oil until golden brown. Blend in a ½ cup peanut butter, lowering the flame. Add four cups of vegetable stock or broth, coconut milk and red chillies. Bring to a boil and season to taste with salt and pepper. Finally, lower the heat and let simmer for ten minutes.

— The Spice Of Life —

Ensuring that a dish transcends the ordinary involves a certain alchemy, often dependent on the use of herbs and spices. No less reliant on the power (either real or imagined) of spices was the preparation of stimulants, magic potions, perfumes, offerings to fertility gods, amulets and ointments.

Discovered by explorers, many herbs and spices came (and still come) from far off lands and have long possessed the reputation of being luxurious, sensuous and most importantly exotic.

Forbidden Herbs & Spices

Since Roman times, herbs and spices have been perceived as an indulgence and as such, many were forbidden. In *The German Encyclopaedia of Folk Medicine* of 1843 by Georg Freidrich Most, it was argued that *spice abuse* lead to the perversion of the young. This idea was echoed by American John Harvey Kellogg. Excessive spice-taking could awaken premature sexual desire leading to masturbation. The Charitable Barefoot Sisters of the Poor held similar fears and helpfully provided a blacklist of those spices deemed worthy of being censored.[70]

Anise (*Pimpinella anisum*)
The Romans used anise with other herbs to flavour cakes eaten at the end of large meals or as an ingredient in wedding cakes.

Basil (*Ocimum basilicum and Ocimum minimum*)
This fragrant member of the mint family has an alluring aroma and a warming effect on the body, promoting circulation. In some parts of Italy, basil is a love token.

Bay Leaf (*Laurus nobilis*)
Roman heroes were crowned with laurel leaves, a symbol of virility.

Borage (*Borago officinalis*)
Used as an abortificant by the Mapuche Indians of Chile, in moderation Borage is said to stimulate desire.

---

70 Allende, Isabel *Aphrodite, A Memoir of the Senses* Flamingo 1998, p. 73

Capers (*Capparis spinosa*)

Cardamom (*Elettaria cardamomum*)

Cayenne (*Capsicum frutescens*)

Cinnamon (Cinnamomum zeylanicum and Cinnamomum cassia)

Cinnamon has a fragrant smell, aromatic taste and long history as aphrodisiac.

> I have perfumed my bed with myrrh, aloes and cinnamon.
> Come let us take our fill of love.
> – Proverbs 7: 17-18

Clove (*Eugenia aromatica*)

Cumin (*Cumin cymimum*)

*Caraway[71]

Caraway is often used as a component in aphrodisiac foods, love potions and later in alcoholic beverages.

Chervil

An herb noted for its pleasant, warm and fragrant flavour, chervil resembles myrrh and is used on Holy Days as a symbol of new life. Pliny

---

71 Those herbs marked with as * do not appear in the list of the Charitable Barefoot Sisters.

believed it reinvigorated the body when exhausted by sexual excesses, stimulated the enfeebled powers of old age.

*Chilli

Known as 'Mouth fire', chilli contains the chemical 'capsaicin' that can induce the release of endorphins to create a temporary high. Capsaicin also speeds up the metabolism and increases circulation, responses that are similar to those experienced when having sex. It ignites our internal engine and stimulates our appetite for passion. Eating large quantities of capsaicin may also work as an irritant to the genitals and urinary tract that can feel similar to sexual excitement.

Following an epidemic of prison rapes in the 1970s, the Peruvian government banned chillies from penitentiaries explaining that they were 'not appropriate' for men forced to live a 'limited lifestyle.'[72]

Dill (*Anethum graveolens*)

---

72 Hospodar, Miriam *Aphrodisiac Foods, Bringing Heaven to Earth* Gastronomica, the Journal of Food and Culture Vol.4, p. 91

Fenugreek (*Trigonella forenumbraecum*)
Fenugreek has a repugnant odor and for centuries was believed by Europeans to inflame 'low' passions (i.e. lust) and provoke sensual dreams.

*Garlic

> There are two Italies… The one is the most sublime and lovely contemplation that can be conceived by the imagination of man; the other is the most degraded, disgusting, and odious. What do you think? Young women of rank actually eat – you will never guess what – garlick! Our poor friend Lord Byron is quite corrupted by living among these people, and in fact, is going on in a way not worthy of him.
> – Percy Bysshe Shelley, in a letter from Naples (22 December 1818)

This hot, pungent condiment is said to stir sexual desires and Roman priestesses of old claimed garlic could make 'women fall in love and men powerful.' It is certainly an immensely healthy food with many disease-protective qualities such as lowering cholesterol, aiding circulation and fighting bacteria, fungi and viruses. The problem with garlic is its potent aroma. Pliny (1st century), Roman scholar, identified garlic in any form to be an aphrodisiac but best taken with chopped coriander leaves in white wine.

Ginger (*Zingiber officinale*)

Within the stomach, loins and in the lung
Praise of hot ginger rightly may be sung
It quenches thirst, revives, excites the brain
And in old age awakes young love again[73] .

Ginseng

Ginseng is an oft-used aphrodisiac in Asian cultures, but American researchers remain sceptical of its powers. Ginseng means 'Man root', and has been shown to get animals aroused, but these results have not been duplicated in studies with human subjects.

Lavender (*Lavendula angustifolia*)
Lemon Balm (*Melissa officinalis*)

* Liquorice

Research has revealed that the smell itself is particularly stimulating. A study by Dr Hirsch, the neurological director of the Smell and Taste Treatment and Research Foundation in Chica-

---

73 Ekdah, Raviez Marilyn, *Erotic Cuisine, A Natural History of Aphrodisiac Cookery* Xlibrus Corporation, 2000, p. 124

go, has shown that black liquorice increased the blood flow to the penis by 13 per cent. It is also said to contain traces of the female sex hormone oestrogen and was used medicinally before beginning to be eaten as a sweet.

Liquorice was used in ancient China for its love and lust-provoking properties. The Brahmans of Ancient India used it as a beautifying agent and sexual tonic. Ancient Egyptians saw it as a stimulant; indeed Tutankhamun was buried with a piece of liquorice root as an assist in the future world.

Mint (Mentha veridis mentha rotundifolia)
Shakespeare refers to it along with lavender and rosemary as a stimulant for middle-aged gentlemen.

Mustard (Brassica mugre and sinapsis alba)

Nutmeg (Myristica fragrans)
Nutmeg has been lauded as an aphrodisiac across numerous cultures and is particularly prized by Chinese women. However, large quantities of nutmeg can be psychoactive and produce hallucinogenic effects.

Oregano (*Origanum vulgare and orianum onite*)
Parsley (*Petroselinum crispum*)
Pepper (*Piper migrum*)

Saffron (*Crocus sativus*)
Considered an aphrodisiac by the Arabs, Indians and Chinese.

Sage (*Salvia officinalis*)
Hippocrates (4th century BC), Father of Modern Medicine, prescribed sage for increasing the sexual appetite of women.

Tarragon (*Artemisa dracunculus*)
Thyme (*Thymus vulgaris*)
Tumeric (*Curcuma longa*)

Vanilla (*Vanila fragans vanilla planifolia*)
The Elizabethans regarded vanilla as wickedly aphrodisiacal because the pod of the plant resembled the vagina. The actual word dervives from the Spanish for 'little vagina'. Brillat -Savarin recommended a most divine sounding dessert called 'pyramid of vanilla and rose meringues'. Ironically, these days 'vanilla sex' refers to bland and ordinary sex.

Over-Stimulating Herbs

Those Barefoot Sisters may have had a point as there are some very effective aphrodisiacal herbs which, without appropriate instruction, can have detrimental side-effects. These include Yohimbe Bark, Centrum Damiana (or just Damiana), Muira Puama, Pregnenolone (Mexican Yam), Maca (Lepidium meyenii), Horny Goat Weed and to a milder extent Ginkgo Biloba.

Mandrake

Mandrake is a root plant that can be traced back to the Bible and has been credited with promoting desire and fertility since Leah used mandrake to charm Jacob into her bed. Plutarch and Pliny the Elder both mentioned mandrake root's resemblance to a penis and testicles. The Egyptians called it the 'Phallus of the field' and the Hebrew name for mandrake is *pleasures of love*. St Hildegard of Bingen wrote in the 12th century, 'In mandragora the influence of the Devil is more present than in other herbs consequently man is stimulated by it according to his desires whether they be good or bad.' Machiavelli is much more enthusiastic: 'You must know,' he wrote, 'that nothing is so sure to make women conceive as a draught composed of mandragora. This is a fact which I have verified upon 4 occasions.'[74] It was believed that mandrake sprang up beneath the gallows where criminals, especially rapists, ejaculated sperm or urinated the instant they died.

Epimedium

Known as Horny Goat Weed (among many other aliases), Epimedium is an umbrella term for a genus comprising 60 species. It is largely endemic to southern China, and is said to treat fatigue and improve sexual function by altering specific hormone levels.

Yohimbe, Tribulus and Maca

There are several traditional herbs under study for their aphrodisiac properties, and three leading contenders are Yohimbe, Tribulus and Maca. Any combination of these might be pulverized, capsulated and sold as 'natural Viagra'. However, too much Yohimbe, a bark from a West African evergreen tree, can kill – not the kind of stiffness most seek.

---

74 Hendrickson, Robert *Lewd Food: The Complete Guide to Aphrodisiac Edibles* Chilton Book Company, 1974, p. 290

— Venerous Veg —

Asparagus

Blatantly phallic and famously aphrodisiacal, the asparagus contains potassium, fibre, vitamins B6, A and C, thiamin and folic acid. The latter is said to boost histamine production, necessary to reach orgasm in both sexes. Asparagus 'stirs up lust in man and woman', wrote English herbalist Nicholas Culpepper in the 17th century.

A popular sexual metaphor and visual innuendo on a par with the banana, our love affair with this member of the Lily family dates back hundreds of years. Its potency has been recorded on the page from early Greek times and expressed in the literature of China and of India, whose *Kama Sutra* advised that 'the drinking of a paste composed of the asparagus is a provocative of sexual vigour'.

In the 1932 film *Young Ironsides*, it is used for comic effect to signify impotence. When Charley Chase attempts to eat asparagus it wilts, bends and continues to do so at his every attempt. Even when his girlfriend tries to grasp it at the stalk, it does not rise.

In 19th century France, bridegrooms were served three courses of the sexy spears at their prenuptial dinner.

Avocado or Alligator pear

A fruit of the 'Ahuacuatl' or 'testicle tree' Aztecs thought the avocado resembled the male testicles as they hung in pairs. It is said that the first Europeans to taste the green flesh were Cortez and his conquistadores.

The Spanish found avocados so obscenely sexy that Catholic priests forbade them to their parishioners. The creamy fruit is especially good for pregnant women for its high content of folic acid, vitamin B6 and potassium. They are also said to boost the immune system. Louis XIV had a taste for 'bonne poire' as he called it, believing it rejuvenated his ageing libido.

Tomatoes or Love Apples

Another culinary discovery courtesy of Cortez was the tomato. He brought it from Mexico to Spain in 1520. It is said that the name sprang from a miscommunication. At that time Spaniards were called Moors and it is said a Frenchman served 'pomi des Moro' (Moors' apples) heard 'pommes d'amour', or 'love apples', which is how Sir Walter Raleigh then described them upon presenting one to Queen Elizabeth.

Hence, this exotic new fruit/vegetable (botanically a fruit but legally a vegetable) came to be regarded as an aphrodisiac. In Germany, it is still known as *liebesapfel*, a love apple. The tomato's reputation as a wickedly powerful sexual stimulant had virtuous maidens all a-quiver. The non-virtuous, who flagrantly indulged in the flesh of the fruit, were hence branded 'hot tomatoes'. 'Love Juice' or Ketchup according to the *Oxford English Dictionary* dates back to 1711.

The tomato plant is a member of the deadly nightshade family. In his commentaries *The Six Books of Dioscorides* (1544), the Italian herbalist Pier Andréa linked the tomato with the mandrake, Bella Donna and other poisonous plants containing dangerous alkaloids, and it was consequently condemned in the US by the Puritans. These dangerously wicked 'wolf peaches' were forbidden and marked with a skull and crossbones.

It was only in 1820 that the tomato's benign nature was finally accepted when Colonel Robert Gibbon Johnson proved the authorities wrong.

On September 26th, he appeared on the steps of the Salem Court New Jersey ready to eat a whole basket of 'wolf peaches'. Two thousand people had gathered, convinced he would be poisoned to death and a dirge played as he ate from the basket.

'The foolish colonel will foam and froth at the mouth and double over with appendicitis. All that oxalic acid,' cried Dr. James Van Meeter (Johnson's own physician).

Nevertheless, Johnson ate on. 'The time will come,' he declared, 'when this luscious, golden apple, rich in nutritive value, a delight to the eye, a joy to the palate whether fried, baked, grilled or eaten raw will be recognized, eaten and enjoyed as an edible food.'

Artichokes
Dr Nicolas Venette (1633-1698) stated in his book *Tableau de l'amour Conjugal*, that the globe artichoke produces much semen and vigour. Regarded as a warming food, Parisian vendors would cry out, 'Artichokes! Artichokes! Heats the body and the spirit! Heats the Genitals!'

The pioneer of the exotic
– erotic morphology of the artichoke

> I seek in anonymity's cloister
>
> Not him who ate the first raw oyster but one who,
>
> Braving spikes and prickles
>
> The spine that stabs the leaf that tickles
>
> With infinite patience and fortitude
>
> Unveiled the artichoke as food.
>
> – Ogden Nash

Aubergine or Eggplant

Considered a most effective aphrodisiac, aubergine was served daily to the Turkish sultan and remains a popular vegetable in Turkish cuisine. Apparently, the good women of Turkey pride themselves on knowing at least fifty recipes for this vegetable.

The most canny of all Turkish wives was surely Rada who served her husband, the legendary Turkish bey Mustaph Mehere (1488-1611), a highly potent aubergine dish, the recipe of which she kept secret. Rada was one of his 170 wives and innumerable concubines. Her husband, who weighed 400 lbs, is said to have lived to be 123 years old and had the habit of discarding all his wives once they reached the age of twenty. However, Rada was kept alive for her secret dish. [75]

The *Kama Sutra* suggests that 'If the lingam is rubbed with the fruit juices of the eggplant amongst other things, a swelling lasting for a month will be produced'.

In contrast, John Gerard warned in the *Herball* (1597) that 'I rather wish English men to content themselves with the meat and sauce of our own country – doubtless these apples have a mischievous quality; the use whereof is utterly to be forsaken'.[76] Describing it as the *mad apple*, he claimed it could cause insanity.

Beans

My love hung limp beneath the leaf
(O bitter bitter shame)
My heavy heart was full of grief
Until my lady came.
She brought a tasty dish to me
(O swollen pod and springing seed!)
My love sprang outright eagerly

75 Lewd food Hendrickson, Robert *Lewd Food: The Complete Guide to Aphrodisiac Edibles* Chilton Book Company, 1974, p. 208

76 Ibid, p. 207

To serve me in my need.

– From an old English Ballad entitled *The Love Bean*[77]

Regarded as a spur to love, beans were held in high esteem by the Romans, so much so that the leading families of the day named themselves after these haricots. The Roman Fabii took their name from fada (bean), the Lentuli took theirs from the lentil and even the great house of Cicero was named after chickpea. It was believed that foods (like baked beans, rich in iron, copper and phosphorus) were potent because they enabled men to attain prodigious erections by means of their eruptions or accumulated gas.

In Honas Province along the Yellow river in China, carp and red bean soup is regarded as an indispensable dish for newlyweds.

Chick Peas
In North African countries, chickpeas are employed extensively in cooking. Many believe that they increase the energy and sexual desires of both men and women. In al-Nafzawi's *The Perfumed Garden*, chickpeas are recommended as a cure for impotence and a first-rate sexual stimulant.

77 Ibid, p. 200

Abu el-Heidja has deflowered in one night
Once eighty virgins, and he did not eat or drink between,
Because he surfeited himself with chickpeas,
And had drunk camel's milk with honey mixed.
– Sheik Nefzawi *The Perfumed Garden*

In the Indian sex manual *Ananga Ranga* a recipe for chickpea cake is given, which, if eaten every morning... will allow one to 'be able to enjoy a hundred women.'

Carrots – What's up Doc?

Symbolically phallic, the Japanese have a variety of carrot that grows to three feet long. John Gerard, 16th century botanist and author, claimed in his celebrated 'Herball' (1597) that carrots were helpful in 'love matters'.

Celery

Visually suggestive but also regarded as a remedy for impotence, the Greeks held celery in such esteem that they awarded a stalk to the winners of their nude athletic events. The Romans also favoured the abilities of this vegetable and dedicated celery to Pluto, the 'god of sex'.

The Swedish author C.E. Hagdahl in his *Cooking as Science and Art* (1879) writes, 'Celery contributes to a stimulation of the digestion, but is also suspected to be somewhat sexually exciting or even straightforward arousing.'

Grimod de la Reyniere, in his *Almanach des Gourmands* (1803) agreed: 'It is not a salad for bachelors...'

Eryngoes and Sea Vegetables

Eryngoes grow wild along the coast of England and are cultivated for their medicinal elements. Known as Kissing Comfits, as they create a thirst for more kissing, they look like a thistle with a blue flower. Rich in iodine, the roots are said to excite and strengthen the genitalia of both sexes.

Ancient Greek physician Dioscordes mentioned them as an aid to digestion in the first century A.D. and English poet and dramatist John Dryden describes libertines as those 'who wildly dancing at the midnight ball for hot eryngoes and fat oysters call!'

In Jim Crace's *The Devil's Larder*, a couple spot some whilst out walking in the dunes and decide to try them, using a recipe from their cookbook, *Mrs Caraway*. She warns her readers, 'the roots should be first candied or infused with fruits and then consumed. It will be witnessed how quickly

Venus is provoked.'

A meal is duly cooked and the couple awaits the effects...[78]

Fennel

To eat conger eel and fennel was to the Elizabethans intensely provocative. Thus, Shakespeare has Falstaff say of another character 'he plays at quoits well and eats conger and fennel and rides the wild mare with the boys.'

Fennel's aphrodisiac qualities have been scientifically proven – at least in the libido of male and female rats. This is likely due to the hormone-like compounds it contains which mimic the female hormone estrogen. This estrogenic activity is why fennel has been used as a breast enlarger.

Leeks

Another visually stimulating vegetable, Rabelais uses the leek to great comic effect in a scene when Panurge is asked by Friar John about his age. The friar wonders that when there is snow on the mountain (i.e. when one is white-haired), there is not then any considerable heat to be expected in the valleys and Low Countries of the

78 Jim Crace, *The Devils Larder* Viking, 2001, p. 41

codpiece. Panurge strongly defends his virility by comparing it to the leek:

> Thou twittist me with my grey hairs, yet considerest not how I am of the nature of leeks, which with a white head, carry a green, fresh, straight and vigorous tail.

A Whiff of Love:
Garlic, Chives, Onions, Leeks, Shallots...

> If your wife is old and member is exhausted eat onions in plenty... in the same way should your anus languish do not cease eating of bulbs and Charming Venus will once more smile on your forays. [79]
>
> – Roman poet and epigrammatist, Martial

The onion was long believed to increase the production of sperm and in the *Perfumed Garden*, we are told about the member of a certain Abou el Heiloukh, that remained erect for 30 days because he did eat onions.

About garlic, Ovid wrote in the *Art of Love*, 'She whose breath is strong smelling should never talk with an empty stomach; and she should always stand at distance from her lover's face.'

---

79 Hendrickson, Robert *Lewd Food: The Complete Guide to Aphrodisiac Edibles* Chilton Book Company, 1974, p. 211

This is every cook's opinion
No savory dish without an onion,
But lest your kissing should be spoiled
Your onions must be fully boiled.
– Jonathan Swift (1667-1745)

Molokai

Molokai (Jews Mellow), a popular green in the Middle East, was considered a sexual stimulant that made women stray into the arms of strange men. As such, Al-Hakim bi-'Amr Allah, a Caliph of Egypt in the 10th and 11th centuries, banned it for fear of its potency.

Loose Morels

The ancient Greeks dedicated mushrooms to the God of Love and as far as the Egyptians were concerned, they were only for the lips of Pharaohs. The Chinese called them the divine fruit of immortality and the Aztecs thought they were God's own flesh.

Some 50,000 varieties of mushroom exist and they are mentioned in the erotic cookery of almost every country, Oriental and Occidental.

17th century Potatoes

Shakespeare described the potato as 'finger of the devil luxury' (slang for a dildo or penis) and had Falstaff in *The Merry Wives of Windsor* 'rain potatoes and snow Eryngoes'.

Radish

Known also as Winter Roses, radishes were used in ancient Rome as part of a traditional punishment for sexual offences such as adultery, whereby it was inserted into the offender's anus.

(Lady) Garden Salad

Casanova depicts a garden in a famous Parisian bordello 'so arranged it could serve all the joys of love'. Rabelais wrote about salads 'wholly made up of Venerous herbs and fruits, such as rocket, tarragon, cresses, parsley, rampions, poppy, celery.'

Martial in his writings referred to the aphrodisiac quality of the salad vegetable 'rocket', which was planted around shrines dedicated to the phallic god, Priapus.

Scallions lustful rockets nought prevail
And heightening meats in operation fail
Thy wealth begins the pure cheeks to defile
So, venery provoked lives but while;
We can admire enough, the wonders such
That thy not standing stands thee in so much.[80]

---

80 Martial Epigram (3.75) McLaren, Angus, Impotence, A Cultural History, University of
Chicago Press 2007, p. 21

— Fetishistic Foods —

For those with a more adventurous palate, the following aphrodisiacs span the range from the downright cruel to the monstrously revolting. Amongst the contenders are pubic hairs baked in bread[81], a type of Bloody Mary which contains ingredients suggested by its name, baked sparrow[82], and bowels of the Blue Jay. A popular Ancient Roman orgy food was dormice sprinkled with honey and poppy seeds.[83] In Chile, there is spider that lives in the sea urchin, which is traditionally eaten whilst still alive. Placed on the tip on the tongue it is gently crushed to death up against the roof of one's mouth. In medieval China, jade was believed to be the congealed sperm of dragons and so crushed into powder for use in love potions. But the most gory of all aphrodisiacs is surely cannibalism.

---

81 Take three pubic hairs and three from the left armpit. Burn them on a hot shovel. Pulverize and insert into a piece of bread. Dip bread in a soup and feed to lover, according to Albert Magnus medieval philosopher.

82 Cyranus, ancient king of Persia warrants that baked sparrow dissolved in a liquid is apparently a sure way to make woman melt away for love.

83 Apicius' recipe for Dormouse, 'Slit open and gut four dormice and stuff them with a mixture of minced pork and dormouse (all parts) pepper, nuts, stock and laser (a wild African fennel). Stitch up and roast on a tile or in a small clay oven. Satyricon coated them with honey and poppy seeds.

Bird's Nest Soup

This is an Asian delicacy renowned for its ability to stimulate the libido, made from the nests of swallows (a bird believed to coit on the wing). [84] The nests used are from two different types of swallow. Nests from the cave dwelling swallow are to be found in the limestone caves of Borneo. These caves are inhospitable and dangerous labyrinths, full of bats, birds and huge deposits of guano. These nests resemble glutinous half cups composed of fish spawn, seaweed and bound together by the birds cement-like saliva.

The nests of the Sea Swallow are found high up on cliffs along the Annam coast of Java and a few other Malayan Islands. When the birds start nesting and just before the mating season their swollen saliva glands produce a thick white, liquid composed principally of nitrogenous matter (including seaweed and fish spawn) that is insoluble in water. Lengths of this sticky saliva dribble from the bird's beak and then layered one atop the other to make the nest.

Roman Fish Sauce

Known as Garum, muria or liquamen, this sauce

---

84 Hendrickson, Robert *Lewd Food: The Complete Guide to Aphrodisiac Edibles* Chilton Book Company, 1974, p. 20

was as popular as today's ketchup. It is thought to have tasted like a cross between anchovy paste and current South East Asian fish sauces. Extremely flavoursome, Garum was made from the blood, gills and intestines of fish, which were heavily salted and placed in vats in the sunlight for several weeks.

Shark Fin Soup

'Eat and await love's call,' cry the Chinese about their beloved Yerchee or shark fin soup. Alas, for the declining shark population.

Puffer Fish

The puffer fish or Fugu is a deadly aphrodisiac enjoyed by the Japanese. Highly toxic, it can only be prepared by a licensed Fugu chief and it is estimated that about 300 people die annually from eating Fugu.

Cyanide is like mothers' milk in comparison to the Fugu poison, for an ounce of serotoxin poison can kill 56,000 diners.

Apparently, the taste causes the mouth to feel numb. As the numbness wears off there is a lingering tingle on the lips and inside the cheeks. This tingling is said to greatly promote sexual arousal. If unlucky enough to be poisoned, the victim falls into a paralyzed death-like state, unable to communicate. A slow painful demise ensues, although there have been incidences of miraculous recovery. Indeed, it is now the custom to wait a least a few days before burying the victim, just in case they are buried alive.

Cats and Dogs

Cat and dog are both well-liked meats by the Chinese. The 1920s Chinese warlord Chang Chungch'ung is said to have eaten black chow meat (dog) daily. The Dog Meat General, as he came to be called, relied on it for his strength as he famously used to take on whole Shanghai brothels at a time. Dog was also a favourite of the Aztecs who raised a breed of hairless Chihuahuas specifically for eating.

Dog à la Beti

Ingredients

One dog

Small leaved basil

Skin of a garlic plant

Sweet Banana (Odoze Beti variety)

Pepper

Citronella

'Odjom'

Onions

Banana leaves

Method

This recipe requires a few preliminaries. Before being killed, the dog should be tied to a post for a day and hit with small sticks to shift the fat in the adipose tissue. After killing, it is cut up into chunks. The skin is scorched over a fire and scraped with a knife. The bowels are emptied, cleaned and rolled up. The pieces of meat are washed and scraped several times until there is no trace of blood or dirt left in the water. The stiff main veins of the banana leaves are skinned, and then softened over a fire. The leaves are placed in a criss-cross fashion in a big pan. The pieces of meat are mixed with all the condiments in a separate pan. This seasoned meat and some sweet banana of the Odzoe beti variety are placed on the prepared leaves. The leaves are tied together with banana fiber to make a packet. This packet is braised in a pot whose base has been covered with banana leaves. Water is added only up to the mid point so that it cannot penetrate the packet during the cooking.

Cooking the packet takes eight to nine hours, once done the food is served immediately. It is a noble dish reserved for the elders of the village. The sweet bananas absorb the fat exuded by the chunks of meat in the course of its cooking. Bananas so prepared are considered succulent. This recipe comes from Cameroon.[85]

Camel Toes...
(perhaps a crass innuendo but no need to get the hump!)

Love potions made from burnt camel bone and fat from the camel hump were popular aphrodisiacs in Arabia. Women were advised to rub their genitals with a piece of linen spread with camel marrow. Stuffed camel was traditional fare for a Bedouin Wedding feast and would include a gross of eggs, plus a glean of fish, plus a coop of chickens, all stuffed first into a large sheep and then into a camel. The ancient Romans had a liking for grilled camel's feet. The French are partial to the meat and the *Larousse Gastronomique*

85 Lucan, Medlar, Gray, Durian *The Decadent Cookbook* Dedalus, 2009, p. 121-122

(1961 edition) includes several recipes. During the 1870 siege of Paris, camel appeared on the Christmas Eve menu of the famous Voisin restaurant.

Monkey Love & More Miscellaneous Belly turners...

Roast monkey stuffed with peanuts is a Nigerian favourite. Monkey lips are highly esteemed in India and the Kama Sutra recommends monkey excrement mixed with various ingredients be thrown into the face of one's desire, whom it is said will immediately succumb, although perhaps 'surrender' might be a more apt description.

Apparently, Penis of Hedgehog gave the Romans brio. Insects have always been popular: honey-coated bumblebees, stuffed South American beetles, breaded pallor worms, crickets, roast caterpillar, fried grass hopper, locusts (a favourite of some Arabs), cicadas (Aristotle loved them) and sun-dried termites. For those epicureans whose curiosity and palate is tickled by such thoughts see Dr F. S. Bodenheimer's Insects as Human Food or the 1885 book by V.M. Holt, Why not eat insects?

A Most Foul Fowl Love Potion

One may be smitten by lark's tongues, swallows heart, or even a roast swan. To protect the swan from extinction (due to over eating) in the 12th century the English monarchy decreed royal ownership of all mute swans.

The 17th century *Lucayos Cookbook* (a family manuscript discovered in the 1950s and published for the first time in 1959) describes the following recipe, where pain and pleasure go hand in hand.

> *Take a cock Sparrow and pluck it whilst living then throw it to ten wasps who will sting it to death. Add a Black Ravens intestines and oil of lilac plus chamomile, cook in beef fat till the flesh shreds. Put into a bottle and hold near... Ye shall see marvels.*

Rodent Relish

Trapped in Paris in 1870 during the Prussian siege, politician, author and publisher Henry Laboucherie wrote:

> *...This morning I had a salamis of rats. it was excellent, something between frog and rabbit.* [86]

86 Lucan, Medlar, Gray, Durian *The Decadent Cookbook* Dedalus, 2009, p. 118

Steak a la Tonelier (or rat stew) was at certain times regarded as an invigorating dish. The *Larousse Gastronomique* recommends that the tastiest rats are those found in the wine cellars, perhaps assuming they may be marinated from within.

Entrecote A la Bordelaise

Skin and gut your rat. Rub with a thick sauce of olive oil and crushed shallots. Season with salt and pepper. Grill the meat over a fire of broken wine barrel wood and serve with a Bordelaise sauce.

Horse

Horse penis was very popular meat in medieval times and for ultimate potency, it was cut off in full erection and served in a cream sauce. A horsemeat banquet held at the Grand Hotel in Paris 1852, attended by Dumas, Flaubert, Sainte Beauve and 129 other guests, famously served a menu were every course contained an element of horse meat. Dessert was Rum and horse marrow cake.

Aside from the penis, the *Hippomanes* was considered even more potent. The part of horse it actually referred to has been a matter of some debate. Described by Virgil as a bitter fluid flowing from the vulva of rutting mares, it is probably (and as suggested by Ovid, Juvenal and Pliny), the black or brown Caul that appears on a foal's head at birth, resembling a fig. The mare bites it off before she gives milk to her offspring. It is said Caligula was thrown into frenzy when given it by his wife.

Meat Balls

Testicles from a multitude of animals have been used as aphrodisiacs including tenderised tiger testicles, ostrich testicles, mountain goats' testicles. But top of all testicles are the bullock's.

Known as Bulls Balls, Rocky Mountain Oysters, Prairie Oysters and Spanish Kidneys, these testicles have always been a symbol of virility. 'Strong like a bull' is a phrase that attracts some lovers to this four-legged mammal with a notorious temper. In areas of Southeast Asia, a soup (known as soup #5) composed of onions, carrots, broth and bull's penis and testicles is a popular dish noted for its aphrodisiac properties.

Bull urine was recommended as an aphrodisiac by ancient Roman writer Paulinus and bull dung featured in love recipes of the Navajo Indians. However far more appetising was the recipe for Pie of Bulls Testicles, invented by Bartolomo Scappi, chef to Pope Pius V. in the 16th century.

Bollock Stew

(from an 18th century erotic cookbook)

'Boil the testicles in salted water, let them cool, peel off the skin, finely dice the meat and mix with onions, fried minced calf liver, and bacon. Season generously with rosemary clove cinnamon salt and pepper and cover with a thick wine sauce and use as a filling for a meat pie.' [87]

Rhino Horn

The 16th century Chinese female poet Huang O wrote that when she and her lover shared a piece of magic rhino horn, the whole night long she clung 'trembling to the flower stamen'.

While the horns of several animals, including those of the unicorn, have been touted as aphrodisiacs over the centuries, perhaps the most famous myth is that belonging to the rhino horn. This myth has persisted in Western cultures despite significant educational efforts made by the

---

87 Allende, Isabel *Aphrodite, A Memoir of the Senses* Flamingo 1998, p. 95

World Wildlife Federation and other organizations due to the near extinction of the animal. In fact, rhino horn is used in Traditional Chinese Medicine to treat fever, high blood pressure, and other illnesses, but *not* as an aphrodisiac. Rhino horn from Asian and Africa used for these 'medicinal' purposes, commands thousands of dollars per pound, despite being an illegal product. As always the illicit aspect lends it a more mysterious edge.

Snakes

Snakes have sexual connotations that go back centuries. Fresh snake blood and sugar stirred into liquor is an esteemed stimulant in Taiwan and other Asian countries. Isabelle Allende refers to an account from a San Francisco paper where a group of Malaysian Chinese immigrants drank rattlesnake blood. 'They opened a slit in the tail and while one person held the snake by the head and squeezed downward to drain it, the other lay on the ground and sucked the blood between swigs of whiskey'.[88]

Cobra meat is also eaten for its aphrodisiac qualities. Robert Ripley of *Ripley's Believe it or Not!* fame attributed his renowned virility largely to

88 Allende, Isabel *Aphrodite, A Memoir of the Senses* Flamingo 1998, p. 173

a diet that regularly included such delicacies as rattle snake ragout.

Cordyceps

Historically known as caterpillar fungus or dong chong Xia cao in China, cordyceps was revered in the East as an aphrodisiac extraordinaire. This fungus is a parasite of sorts; it invades the brains of caterpillar larva and grows there eventually replacing native tissue with its own. Today it is cultivated so that it can be purchased quite in-expensively unlike many other bizarre culinary aphrodisiacs.

Balut

A popular Asian dish is a duck egg that contained a fetus, something which is said to have Via-gra-like properties. The egg is simply boiled and served. Once the fetus or embryo is consumed, the stimulation is thought to begin.

Skink

The skink is a North African lizard that from times as remote as Greek and Roman antiquity has been said to have fantastic aphrodisiac pow-ers. The snout, feet and genitals are soaked in wine and cooked in a bed of herbs. The Persians mixed the flesh of the skink with ground pearls and amber. It is said the Arabs liked powdered lizard whilst the South Americans liked iguana lizard.[89]

---

89 Hendrickson, Robert *Lewd Food: The Complete Guide to Aphrodisiac Edibles* Chilton Book Company, 1974, p. 97

Excretions

Musk

Musk is a pungent substance found in the sex glands of the 20-inch high musk deer that roams the Himalayas and Atlas ranges. The best quality musk comes from Tibet. The deer's scent glands are golf ball sized, covered in hair and found beneath the animal's stomach.

Civet

This is the excretion from the civet cat, a first cousin of the mongoose. Traditionally in Ethiopia, the cats were raised in cages and then beaten to enrage them, so filling their genital scent pouches. This practice has long since ceased and the Civet smell is now chemically produced. A favourite scent ingredient, it was used in perfumes, most famously Channel No. 5.

Give me an ounce of civet good apothecary to sweeten my imagination.

– *King Lear*, Shakespeare

Ambergris

A waxy substance made in the intestines of the sperm whale, ambergris is regarded as a powerful erotic stimulant. Once expelled, it is found floating in the tropics and has been eagerly harvested for many hundreds of years. Ambergris was often used in cookery and in the 17th century chocolates were covered and coffee laced with a smidgeon of this substance. Persians sucked on pastilles containing powdered ambergris. Used as a base for expensive perfumes, it has now been replaced by more accessible chemical components.

Blood

Blood is the quintessential liquid of life. To be hot-blooded is to have too much heat in one's blood and to be extremely passionate. People have ingested the blood of everything in the hope of increasing strength, potency and libido.

Menstrual blood was in the past considered particularly aphrodisiacal. During the Ming Dynasty, Emperor Shih Tsung (1522-1567) kept 460 young virgins on hand to supply him with menstrual blood ensuring his longevity and as an elixir.[90] Even today in New York's Vampire Sex

90 Hospodar, Miriam *Aphrodisiac Foods, Bringing Heaven to Earth* Gastronomica, the Journal of Food and Culture Vol.4, p. 90

Club, evenings are hosted in which participants drink each other's blood.

Excrement

Pliny the Elder mentioned the aphrodisiac properties of faeces in Roman times and they have since been used in many European and Chinese aphrodisiac recipes. A late 17th century formula containing faeces received endorsement from the university faculty of Leipzig, Germany. Today sex play involving faeces is sometimes called a 'fudge party', and anal intercourse, 'the Hershey Highway'.

> The shit was very tasty. I helped myself to as much of it as I had the fish sperm. I would have taken more if the Negroes had not carried it away. The next dish to arrive was stuffed cow's vulva.' So begins L'Anglais Decret dans le Chateau Ferme.
>
> – Andrie Pieryre de Mandiargues,
>
> published by Gallimard L'Imaginaire, 1993

Poisons

Cantharides or Spanish fly

'But this powder,' we said, 'What do they do with it?'
'It's not what they do with it,' the Major said. 'Its what it does to you...'
'... It builds a fire under your genitals it is both a violent aphrodisiac and a powerful irritant. It not only makes you uncontrollably randy but it also guarantees you an enormous and long lasting erection at the same time.'
– Roald Dahl, My Uncle Oswald [91]

'Spanish fly' is a deadly aphrodisiac made from the ground up bodies of a tiny iridescent blister beetle found in Spain and Southern Italy. The beetle contains a caustic acid-like juice called cantharidin. When ingested this toxin causes a burning and swelling sensation in the urinary tract misconstrued as sexual stimulation. It can also cause kidney malfunction, gastrointestinal hemorrhages and death.

Widely used by the most depraved of the European nobility, the Marquis de Sade made the mistake of slipping it into the food of some of

---

91 Dahl, Roald My Uncle Oswald Penguin Books, 1980, p. 12

his conquests, and was convicted, in 1772, under a poisoning charge. Moreau de Tours gives an exaggerated account of what happened to de Sade's unfortunate guests, following a dessert of chocolate flavoured with vanilla and Spanish fly: *'Both men and women were seized with a burning sensation of lustful ardour. The essence of cantharides circulating in their veins left them neither modesty nor reserve, in the imperious pleasure excess was carried to the most fatal extremity; pleasure became murderous, blood flowed upon the floor and the women only smiled at the horrible effects of their uterine rage.'*

Nux Vomica

Italian writer and famed lothario D'Annunzio wrote 'though gifted to excess with organs and glands more suitable to a stallion... (I) have reached my 62nd birthday with a somewhat diminished capacity for the pleasure of the flesh...' So, to sustain his reputation, he self-medicated dangerously: 'Though strychnine may be injurious to lesser men it has proved a boon to me as a virtuoso in the arts of love.' [92]

---

92 Hendrickson, Robert *Lewd Food: The Complete Guide to Aphrodisiac Edibles* Chilton Book Company, 1974, p. 267

I could eat you

A sensuous desire let loose and then overcome by an unbridled passion can be an experience of such physical intensity that we nuzzle, nibble, lick, suck, bite, chew, swallow... Indeed, we may feel desire as an all-consuming love but rarely in the modern world do we actually ingest the flesh of our loved ones.

The Thief: Jesus, God...
His Wife: It is not God Albert. It is Michael, my lover. You vowed you would kill him and you did and you vowed you would eat him, now eat him.

In Peter Greenaway's film of 1989 *The Cook, the Thief, His Wife and her Lover*, the Thief has received his comeuppance and is forced to eat his wife's lover. This is a film obsessed with human corporeality, with eating, drinking, defecating, urinating, copulating, belching, vomiting, spitting and bleeding, and so intertwined are the elements that the audience is equally repulsed and seduced despite the aesthetic visual brilliance.

Cannibalism

Cannibalism has been practised by many tribes and cultures over time. Toasting someone with a Nordic 'SKOL' harkens back to Viking times, when skulls were used as cups to drink the blood of their victims.[93]

In Medieval times, victims of cannibalism were often ascribed to werewolves and vampires. De Sade advocated cannibalism when his character Minski fed Juliette her own chambermaid. In his comic masterpiece *Gargantua and Pantagruel*, Rabelais' cited a most pure and soulful Pilgrims Salad which his hero Gargantua makes with six Pilgrims, mixed with lettuce, salt, vinegar and oil.

Joseph Campbell in his book *The Power of Myth* cites a New Guinea cannibalistic ritual where young boys are introduced to sex for the first time. The tribe enters a sacred field where they chant and beat drums for 4 to 5 days and then engage in a sexual orgy.

93 Hendrickson, Robert *Lewd Food: The Complete Guide to Aphrodisiac Edibles* Chilton Book Company, 1974, p. 110

'There is a great shed of enormous logs supported by two uprights... a young woman... lies down beneath the great roof. The boys six or so with the drums going and chanting. Have their first experience of intercourse with the girl. And when the last boy is with her in full embrace, the supports are withdrawn, the logs drop and the couple is killed. There is the union of male and female as they were in the beginning of begetting and death then the couple is pulled out, roasted, and eaten that very evening. The ritual is the repetition of the original act of the killing of a god, followed by the coming of food from the dead savoir.'[94]

The ideal way to prepare human flesh is by slow stewing rather than spit roasting according to those who have sampled this dish, whom include Guy de Maupassant, Marco Polo and Captain James Cook (the latter was eventually eaten himself). [95]

---

94 P 137 Ackerman, Diane *A Natural History of the Senses* Phoenix Paperback 1996, p. 137
95 Daniel rogue Film Food sitehttp://www.londonfoodfilmfiesta.co.uk/FILMMAffi1/Foodfiffi1.htm

How to eat an Adult

I like mine toasted
Slow roasted
Topped with sesame seeds
Or filleted
Bread crumb-ed
Fried in sizzling grease
Eyes are delicious
Noses a treat
The flesh behind knees
I find rather sweet.
Fingers are crunchy
Thighs are delice
Baked heart with sliced liver
A wonderful dish
Shoulder ragout
Is a favourite of mine
Lips a la flambe
Is rather sublime
Quick and easy are ears sauteed in oil
Or baked bottom cheeks wrapped up in foil.
Oh I do love an adult
Simple to cook
Delicious to savour
A treat for the tongue
That robust earthy flavour...

Mmmmm.......
I tell you my friends
It's true what they say
To stay healthy and strong
Have an adult a day

– Lana Citron

— Lip Libations —

Let him kiss me with kisses of his mouth for thy love is better than wine
— *The Song of Solomon*

Of all earthly intoxicants, alcohol reigns supreme in popularity, if not effectiveness, when used correctly in the grand game of seduction. The ayurvadic text the *Astanga Hridaya* recommends that 'at night wine should be consumed twice or thrice in little quantities just to please the woman'.[96]

The process of distillation was first discovered by the Arabs who developed the technique, naming the spirits of the wine 'alkuhul'. In ancient Greece and Rome, the gods of wine, (ecstasy and eroticism), Bacchus and Dionysus figured prominently in their festivals. Orgiastic celebrations held in their honour allowed the masses to drink and fornicate without restraint. It was a time of libertine excesses, but debauchery led to divine punishment and as we are told in the Old Testament the cities of Sodom and Gomorrah

96 Hospodar, Miriam *Aphrodisiac Foods, Bringing Heaven to Earth* Gastronomica, the Journal of Food and Culture Vol.4, p. 82-93

were duly destroyed.

Mead, a sweet wine made from honey, was the first European alcoholic drink and was imbibed well into the 18th century. Hypocras, a popular medieval and Renaissance beverage intended to stimulate as well as intoxicate, was concocted from a mixture of Burgundy wine, sugar and an array of allegedly lust promoting spices such as ginger, cinnamon and cloves, black pepper and cardamom.

Wine fills the heart with thoughts of love and makes it prompt to catch on fire. All troubles vanish, put to flight by copious draughts.

– Ovid

A little alcohol can indeed warm the spirits and dissolve inhibitions. Physiologically, alcohol causes blood to engorge the genitals, relax the libido and liberate existing or dormant desires. *'Even if you were plain, eyes dimmed by wine would think you beautiful, and night would fling a veil over your imperfections,'*[97] but beware overindulgence, which can cause impotence. Of the seven stages of drunkenness – verbose, grandiose, amorous,

---

97 Ovid, *The Art of Love* (translated by James Michie), The Modern Library Paperback Edition, 2002

bellicose, morose, stuperose and comatose – it is highly advisable to stop drinking at the third.[98]

'Coitus after a heavy bout of drinking is to be avoided,' advises the author of *The Perfumed Garden*. Shakespeare concurs: 'Lechery Sir it provokes and unprovokes, it provokes the desire but it takes away the performance.' (*Macbeth*, Porter to *Macduff* Act. 2 Scene 3.)

In matters relating to alcohol and social etiquette, Ovid counsels the fairer sex that:

> It were better for a young woman to drink, rather than to eat, too freely. Love and wine go very well together. However, do not drink more than your head will stand. Do not lose the use of your head and feet; and never see two things when only one is there. It is a horrible thing to see a woman really drunk. When she is in that state, she deserves to be had by the first comer. When once she is at table, a woman should not drop off to sleep. A sleeping woman is a whoreson temptation to a man to transgress the bounds of modesty.

The following selection of intoxicants have been taken from the drink cabinets of the most famed seducers, wherein lie an array of lip libations.

---

98 Hendrickson, Robert *Lewd Food: The Complete Guide to Aphrodisiac Edibles* Chilton Book Company, 1974, p. 295

Absinthe, or wormwood

A green liqueur extracted from the plant of the same name *Artemisia absinthium* has long been prized for its erotic powers but misused Absinthe can also cause blindness, insanity and death.

Absinthe was invented in 1790 by the French Royalist Dr Pierre Ordinaire, who had fled to Switzerland to escape the Revolution. There he concocted his secret recipe, using absinthium, Spanish anise, star anise, mint-like Melissa, coriander, camomile, veronica, hyssop, persil (parsley) and even spinach. On his death, he passed the recipe into the hands of his son-in-law, Louis Pernod.

Scientists believe that thujone, a constituent of the oil of wormwood, acts as a brain stimulator and aphrodisiac. Traditionally, the bitter-tasting absinthe is sweetened with a lump of sugar and diluted very gradually with water.

It became a French national favourite, enjoyed by libertines, bohemians and artists, many believing it inspired the muses. Famous imbibers include Dumas fils, de Maupassant, Anatole, Verlaine, Rimbaud, Toulouse-Lautrec, Degas, Gaugin, Picasso and Van Gogh, but the ill effects led to its eventual prohibition, in Switzerland in

1908, the US in 1912 and France in 1915.

Amaretto

This is sweet-tasting almond digestive used in cocktails and desserts.

Anise

Anise is used as a base in several aphrodisiac liqueurs such as Pernod, Ricard, Pastis, and *arak*, the national liquor of the Greeks and Turks. Less toxic than absinthe it is a popular drink in France and Spain. Diluted, this transparent drink turns cloudy, perhaps reflecting one's mood when drinking.

Bénédictine

This is an herbal liqueur containing 27 plants and spices. Originally it was developed by the chaste monks of the Benedictine Abbey of Fecamp in Normandy as a medical aromatic herbal beverage. However, the abbey was destroyed during the French Revolution and in 1863, Alexandre Legrand set out to recreate the recipe. Working with a chemist, he developed the formula now in use.

Apparently, the Burnley Miners' Club in Lancashire United Kingdom is the world's biggest single consumer of Benedictine liqueur, after the Lancashire regiments acquired a taste for it during the First World War.[99]

Calvados
An apple brandy from Normandy, calvados has an intense and velvety taste and was regarded as a tonic for staying youthful.

Cachaça
A Brazilian white rum made from fermented sugar cane juice, it is probably the most popular aphrodisiac drink in South America.

Champagne
'Come quickly, I am tasting the stars!' Dom Perignon, when he discovered champagne.

Champagne is synonymous with celebrations. The pop of the cork heralds good times, the fizz – a sensuous smattering of effervescent explosions on the tongue.

This sparkling white wine from the Champagne region of France is more intoxicating than

99 http://en.wikipedia.org/wiki/List_of_QI_episodes_(D_series)#Episode_6_.22Drinks.2

ordinary wine because of its bubbles, which allow the alcohol to enter the blood stream rapidly. Made from the Chardonnay grape, the driest Champagne is of highest value. Champagne is considered a feminine wine and is thought to have a more erotic effect on women than men.

Champagne has the taste of an apple peeled with a steel knife.
– Aldous Huxley (1894-1963)

Cognac, brandy and armagnac

A favoured pre-bedtime tipple of Henry IV, his habit gradually caught on, and from there developed the custom of ending a meal with a cigar and glass of cognac or brandy. This custom does not include the women folk. However, pregnant women have in the past been given a most luxurious supposedly strengthening concoction of brandy beaten with sugar and egg yolk.

Kirsch

Lending colour to sparkling wines, this cherry-based fruit brandy can bring a blush to one's cheeks and is also found in chocolates, cakes and even cheese.

Parfait Amour

This rare lavender-scented liquor had the reputation of being an instant stimulant to the libido and was traditionally served only in the most refined brothels in France.

Vodka

Like whiskey, gin and tequila, vodka is a strong spirit that whilst not specifically an aphrodisiac, does relax inhibitions.

Wine

'Burgundy makes you think of silly things; Bordeaux makes you talk about them, and Champagne makes you do them.'

– Jean-Anthelme Brillat-Savarin

The most divine of all intoxicant alcohols is wine. It adds a further dimension to the pleasure of dining, enhances the atmosphere, relaxes the imbibers and stimulates the senses. The right wines paired with the right food can be a symphony to the palate.

'Hail meat, Praise sauce, And long live wine withal Septembral juices grace our bacchanal to fill the paunch and elevate the cod!'

– Rabelais

'All fine wines must be treated like a lovely woman in bed.' So goes an old Bordeaux proverb, toasted by the Lovers' Clink where arms are entwined and glasses tilted.

The General Sommelier

There are no steadfast rules in achieving the perfect aphrodisical alchemy of wine and food. All is down to personal taste; the following are only general rules of thumb.

Fish and shell fish are best accompanied by a light white, as it is thought that when fish and seafood are mixed with red wine they can leave a bitter taste. Oysters are always good with Chablis. A fuller-bodied white will complement delicate fowl, veal, and strongly flavoured fish like tuna, salmon and meats such as offal.

A crisp rosé is a summer wine for long lunches, or al fresco evenings. A light red might be to your liking with lamb, beef, pork, Italian pasta and organs such as kidney liver and tripe, wild fowl and vegetables. Its more robust sister will flow well with game such as a deer, boar, hare and even some birds like wild duck. Cheese is just the ticket to offset a full-bodied red.

Curries and highly spiced dishes are best with beer and as a general rule the individual cuisine of each country should be accompanied with the drink of the same area, i.e. sake, tea, beer and so on.

Recipe for Love Wine

Take two pints of Chablis, crush an ounce of vanilla beans, cinnamon sticks, dried rhubarb and mandrake or ginseng, add to the wine. Let it stand for two weeks, strain through cheesecloth, add amber and love shall pour forth. [100]

Hardcore Shots

A prodigious aphrodisiac cocktail for those with tastes that are more exotic is gunpowder mixed with rum or whiskey. A drink from the American frontier, cowboys claimed it gave them a certain 'charge'. The microscopic crystals left suspended in the alcohol irritated the urethra and stimulated the erotic processes. [101]

Coffee

The Turks called it 'the black enemy of sleep and copulation'. This argument is maintained

---

100 Hendrickson, Robert *Lewd Food: The Complete Guide to Aphrodisiac Edibles* Chilton Book Company, 1974, p. 292
101 Ibid., p. 301

in *Aphrodisiacs and Anti-aphrodisiacs* where author John Davenport quotes a distinguished British surgeon who confidently declared that 'Any man who drinks coffee and soda water and smokes cigars may lie with my wife.'

In 1674, a remarkable document was published in London entitled *The Women's Petition Against Coffee Representing to Publick Consideration the Grand Inconveniences accruing to their Sex from the Excessive Use of that Drying Enfeebling Liquour.*

It argued that 'Never did Men wear greater Breeches or carry less in them of any Mettle whatsoever... this is due to the Excessive use of that New Fangled abominable heathenish Liquor called Coffee.'

The ladies of the pamphlet promptly received the following response,

> Coffee collects and settles the Spirits, makes the erection more vigorous and the Ejaculation force full adds spiritualescency to the Sperme.[102]

A stimulant rather than an aphrodisiac, French novelist Balzac consumed 50,000 cups of black coffee over a 20-year period. This may have

102 Ellis Aytoun *The Penny Unversities* London Secker and Warburg 1956, p. 88

helped him to produce his numerous master-pieces but it also rotted his stomach and contributed to an early death at 51.

Tea

Brought to Europe by Portuguese merchants from India in 1530, tea had been a refreshing tonic drunk by the Chinese for centuries. A tea syrup was brewed and offered to clients in brothels by prostitutes and was said to have spectacular results.

PART III

— So To The Table &
The Art Of Seduction —

This section of the book presents the reader with a diverse and somewhat erratic selection of aphrodisiacal recipes chosen because they have either appealed, appalled or amused this author's cerebral palate. They may well have been tried and tasted throughout the ages and upon literary pages but I hasten to add the proviso there is no guarantee of effectiveness.

The following 'love' menu comprises **On the Tip of the Tongue**, a collection of love bites, canapés and 'starter' recipes, alongside some saucy soups. **Sweetmeats and Love Feasts** ensues, with a selection of hearty mains (the fripperies and flirtations of the first meeting having dispersed, shifting one's concern to a more steadfast and committed love, remembering well the old adage that the way to a man's heart is through his stomach.) Next, in honour of the courtesans who introduced so many gourmand dishes to the aphrodisiacal repertoire, I offer **a bit on the side.**

Temptation continues with **Happy Ever Afters...** Perhaps desserts are geared toward the fairer sex, but in any case a successful dessert (and for that matter any grand seducer worth his/her title) is one whereby all resistance is futile. By way of an epilogue, there is **the morning after...**

But for now, and to set the tone, let us turn to the Italian Futurists and a page imbued with such romance I was startled by my own appetite...

Declaration of love dinner

A shy lover yearns to express his feeling to a beautiful and intelligent woman. The following *Declaration of Love Dinner* served on the terrace of a grand hotel in the twinkling night of the city will help him to achieve this aim.

I Desire You: antipasto composed of a myriad selection of exquisite tidbits, which the waiter will only let them admire, while She contents herself with bread and butter.

Flesh Adored: A big plate made from a shining mirror, on the centre chicken slices perfumed with amber and covered with a thin layer of cherry jam. She while eating will admire her reflection in the plate.

This is how I will love: Little tubes of pastry filled with many different flavours, one of plums, one of apples cooked in rum, one of potatoes drenched in cognac, one of sweet rice etc. She without batting an eyelid will eat them all.

Super Passion: A very compact cake of sweet pastry with small cavities on the top filled with anise, glacier mints, rum, juniper and Amaro.

Tonight with me: A very ripe orange enclosed in a large hollowed out Sweet pepper embedded in a thick zabaglione flavoured with juniper and salted with little bits of oyster and drops of sea water.[103]

---

103 Tommaso Marinetti (translated by Suzanne Brill) *The Futurist Cookbook* Trefoil Publications Ltd, 1989

— On The Tip Of The Tongue —

As with the exuberant meeting of minds, or attraction of opposites, or glances caught across a room, an amuse bouche (literally a love bite intended to 'amuse the mouth') should excite the appetite, mercilessly tease the taste buds and leave one wanting more (than to be just good friends). Yet, one must take care and not spoil one's appetite by gorging, guzzling or gobbling.

Men became passionately attached to women who cosset them with delicate tidbits.

– Balzac

Canapés (or perhaps for our purposes, 'Love Bites') are intensely flavoured taste explosions too numerous to list in full, but number many containing ingredients you will be familiar with from earlier in this book: Devils on Horseback (prunes wrapped in bacon), Angels on Horseback (shelled oysters concealed in crisp bacon), Russian Quinces stuffed with lamb, savoury tartlets, chicken satay and peanut sauce, delicious morsels of cheese or fruit swathed in parma ham, quail egg croustade, crab toasts, brioches, prawn tempura, rocquefort shortbreads, stuffed majool dates, and a multitudinous variety of vol-au vents. Speaking of which, the ultimate canapé comes courtesy of Antonin Careme, the first celebrity chef, who cooked for all of Europe's royalty and leading families.

Les petits vol- au-vonts a la Nesle Brighton Pavilion and Chateau Rothschild[104]

(or I can't believe how much one can get in a vol- au -vont)

20 vol-au-vent cases,	20 cocks-combs
the diameter of a glass	20 cocks-stones (testes)
10 lambs sweetbreads (thymus and	
pancreatic glands, washed in water	
for five hours, until the liquid runs clear)	
10 small truffles, pared, chopped,	20 tiny mushrooms
boiled in consommé	20 lobster tails
2 tablespoons chopped mushrooms	
4 fine whole lambs' brains,	1 French loaf
boiled and chopped	2 chickens, boned
4 egg yolks	2 spoonfuls chicken jelly

104 Kelly, Ian *Cooking for Kings: The Life of the First Celebrity Chef Antonin Careme*, Short Books Ltd, 2004, p. 259

2 calves' udders

2 pints cream

sauce Allemande

salt, nutmeg

2 spoonfuls velouté sauce

1 tablespoon chopped

parsley

To prepare the Forcemeat:

Crumb a whole French loaf. Add two spoonfuls of
poultry jelly, one of velouté, one tablespoon of chopped
parsley, two of mushrooms, chopped. Boil and stir as it
thickens to a ball. Add two egg yolks. Pound the flesh
of two boned chickens through a sieve. Boil two calves'
udders – once cold, pound and pass through a sieve.
Then, mix six ounces of the breadcrumbs *panada* to ten
ounces of the chicken meat, and ten of the calves' udders
and combine and pound for 15 minutes. Add five drams
of salt, some nutmeg and the yolks of two more eggs
and a spoonful of cold veloute or bechamel. Pound for
a further ten minutes. Test by poaching a ball in boiling
water – it should form soft, smooth balls.

Make some balls of poultry forcemeat in small coffee
spoons, dip them in jelly broth and after draining on a
napkin, place them regularly in the vol-au-vent, already
half filled with: a good ragout of cocks-combs and stones
(testicles), lambs' sweetbreads (thymus and pancreatic
glands, washed in water for five hours, until the liquid
runs clear) truffles, mushrooms, lobster tails, four fine

whole brains. Cover all with an extra thick sauce Allemande.

For the lover with less time on their hands to prepare the above there is nothing wrong with a perfectly glazed cocktail sausage, which few can resist.
Then again one could avoid cooking altogether, raw shashimi, smoked fish, eel, salmon, pâtés, dips, crèmes, foi gras, shot glasses of various potency... or one could just opt for hors d'oeuvres, 'neuf et demi'.

9 ½ Weeks or 'A lucky dip of love...'

Ingredients
Two lusty lovers (**A** & **B**)
One fridge filled with leftovers
One blindfold

Method
Lover **A** blindfolds **B** and feeds **B** various foods. These may include olives, grapes, nuts, dripping honey, yogurt, ice cream, jam, baby tomatoes, cough syrup, and anchovies...

I for one would buckle for **Strawberries Libertes** – fresh giant strawberries hollowed and filled with caviar and sprinkled with vodka.

Ah yes... **Caviar**.
Ideally, expensive caviar should be eaten spooned
directly from its frosty tin and accompanied with chilled
vodka, aquavit or elegant Champagne.

Harlots' Eggs
Mix tablespoons of pimento, anchovy paste, chopped
chives and a dash of lemon juice with one half cup of
caviar.

Petites Croutes de Caviar
Cut out eight round pieces of bread about 1 inch in
diameter and 1.5 inch thick, scooping out the centres
(enough to hold a teaspoon of caviar each).

Caviar is undoubtedly delicious rolled in smoked
salmon and on blinis, sublime. Truman Capote
preferred his in a hot baked potato. Dostoevsky's
wife is said to have regaled him with, on comple-
tion of each chapter of *Crime and Punishment*, fish
eggs and more besides...

And this before we have even sat down.

— So To The Starters —

There are no end of contenders, but nothing quite beats an oyster. Thus I thought I would bring the following passages to your attention. These hail from an 1822 recipe book entitled *The Cooks Oracle.*[105]

On *How to eat an oyster*
– there are some things one just has to know!

Common people, (obviously not speaking about us dear reader) are indifferent about the manner of opening oysters and the time of eating them after they are opened; nothing however is more important in the enlightened eyes of the experienced oyster lover.

Those who wish to enjoy this delicious restorative in its utmost perfection must eat (it) the moment it is opened with its own gravy in the under shell: – if not eaten while absolutely Alive, its flavour and spirit are lost.

---

105 It's full and rather laboured title being: *The cooks oracle containing receipt for plain cookery on the most economical plan for private families also, the art of composing the most simple and most highly finished broths, gravies, soups, sauces, store sauces and flavouring essences.* The quantity of each article is accurately stated by weight and measures the whole being the result of Actual Experiment instituted in The Kitchen of a physician.

The true lover of an Oyster will have some regard for the feelings of his little favourite and will never abandon it to the mercy of a bungling operator, but will open it himself, and contrive to detach the Fish from the shell so dexterously that the Oyster, hardly conscious he has been ejected from his Lodging till he feels the Teeth of the piscivorous Gourmond tickling him to Death.'

That one should hope to die so happy!

Yet it is true nothing can compare to a fresh oyster dressed only in a drop of lemon juice or horseradish or Tabasco sauce. Of course, oysters may be taken many ways; The Cooks Oracle suggests the following:

Scolloped Oysters
Recipe No 182

Stew the oysters slowly in their own liquor for two or three minutes, take them out with a spoon, beard them, and skim the liquor. Put a bit of butter into a stewpan and when it is melted, add as much fine bread crumbs as will dry it up, then put to it the oyster liquor, and give it a boil up, put the oysters into Scollop shells that you have buttered and stewed with bread crumbs, – then a layer of oysters, – then a layer of bread crumbs and then some more oysters, – moisten it with the oyster liquor, cover then with bread crumbs, put about half a dozen little bits of butter on the top of each and brown them in a dutch-oven.

Optional Extras: essence of anchovy, Catsup (Ketchup), cayenne, grated lemon peel, and other spices etc, are added by those who prefer piquancy to the genuine flavour of the oyster. Shrimps may be dressed in the same way.

N.B. Small scollop shells or saucers that hold about half a dozen oysters are the most convenient.

Should oysters fail to delight, you may be more aroused by antipasti, salads, foie gras, chicken liver parfait, pâtés, fondues, stuffed mushrooms, peppers or tortillas. But as a tool of seduction, artichokes are incomparable. Catherine de Medici (1519-1589) had a passion for this spiky vegetable and is credited with having introduced it to France when she married King Henry II at the age of 14.

It has the virtue of... provoking Venus for both men and women; for women making them more desirable, and helping the men who are in these matters rather tardy.

– Dr Bartolomeo Boldo, *Book of Nature*, 1576

The Art of Eating an Artichoke

There is an art to eating an Artichoke. It requires patience and respect. It is a most sensuous experience and one best shared leaf by leaf, as this vegetable is slowly undressed until its very heart is exposed. Each leaf may be dipped in a number of sauces or dressings, which vary from plain to flavoured mayonnaise to pungent salad dressings and vinaigrettes.

Having eaten the leaves one will discover the 'choke', a fibrous, inedible, bristled portion attached to the heart. This choke is easily broken into, scooped out with a spoon, or trimmed off with a knife. The portion that is left is considered the *pièce de résistance*, the heart of the artichoke, a succulent, meaty segment that can be cut into pieces and used in other recipes or simply enjoyed as is, dipped into your favourite sauce.

In 1947 at the Artichoke Festival in Castroville, California, a young woman was crowned 'Miss California Artichoke Queen'. Known to her friends as Norma Jean Baker, she later became screen legend Marilyn Monroe.

For the diehard artichoke connoisseur

When in Rome... a visit to Piperno's is a must for their deep fried artichoke. A Roman Jewish restaurant, its signature dish is this edible flower bud, found at its best in the Roman *campagna*, which is (to quote from the menu) 'thrown into boiling oil, smooth as a billiard ball,' and 'comes out like a chrysanthemum with petals open, distilling its pleasant perfume.'

Or perhaps one could delicately raise your intended's temperature with a savoury flavoursome soufflé. This recipe including radishes, created by chef Alain Lenoir of Boston's Maître Jacques Restaurant, sounds charming. [106]

---

106 Hendrickson, Robert *Lewd Food: The Complete Guide to Aphrodisiac Edibles* Chilton Book Company, 1974, p. 223

Souffle Biochin

Ingredients

12 radishes finely grated

3 tablespoons flour

3 egg yolks well beaten

salt, pepper

3 tablespoons of butter

1 cup whole milk

5 egg whites beaten stiff

Method

Melt butter over a low heat; add flour and blend 3 to 5 minutes. Slowly stir in 1 cup of milk plus any radish juice. Cook and stir sauce with a wire whisk until thick and smooth. Season with salt and pepper. Remove sauce from heat and allow cooling slightly. Add (while stirring) the well-beaten egg yolks and grated radishes. Fold egg whites carefully into mixture. Pour ingredients into 7 inch greased soufflé dish. Bake 25 minutes at 375 F or until set.

The No.1 Aphrodisical Tip?
(Belongs to the Asparagus!)

Madame Pompadour's Asparagus Tips. [107]

For this most regal, delicate and aphrodisical dish you will require **three small bunches of choice asparagus**. The Dutch variety are highly recommended (recognizable by their white stalks and violet heads).

Plunge the stalks into boiling salty water for several minutes. However do not over-cook; they should be firm and upright. A droopy soft asparagus is no good to any one. Each stalk should be cut to 'a little finger's length', and set aside until added to the sauce.

For the white sauce you will need **butter**, a pinch of **salt**, an average spoonful of **spelt flour** and **two fresh yolks** diluted in four spoonfuls of **muscat grape juice**. Cook the sauce in a bain-marie, avoid thickening it too much then add the asparagus tips. The author of the original manuscript observed that this asparagus recipe be served by the spoon and be eaten by the fork.

---

107 http://www.madamedepompadour.com/_eng_pomp/galleria/ditutto/ricette.htm

Nostalgia induces intimacy, a common point of interest between two people. Themed dinners harkening back to childhood days or different eras are always a dinner party favourite.

Retro Starters may be just the nibble to get the party started.

With the 1970s being very much in vogue one could offer up a proliferation of sausage rolls, silverskin onions, cheese straws, stuffed celery, Ritz crackers, devilled eggs, mushroom vol-au-vents, cheese and pineapple on sticks, melon balls, bridge rolls or Coquilles St Jacques, but a huge favourite of that time was...

Prawn Cocktail (you know you want to!)
A simple starter and guilty pleasure this mixture of lettuce, prawns and Marie Rose sauce is the perfect way to start a summer's lunch.

Method

Shred a gem lettuce heart and pile it into a couple of chilled glasses. Peel and dice a cucumber and add it to the lettuce. Mix four tablespoons of decent mayo with two heaped teaspoons of tomato ketchup and a good shake of Tabasco. Toss with 250g plump peeled prawns, a squirt of lemon juice and pinch of paprika. Pile the dressed prawns on top of the lettuce and serve with a lemon wedge balanced on the side of the glass.

— Saucy Soups —
The Ultimate Restorative —

The ultimate restorative is surely soup – everyone knows the healing powers (mental and physical) of comforting chicken soup. But there are soups designed with other sorts of comfort in mind – consommés for consummation, if you will.

Alexandre Dumas père, author of hundreds of novels amongst which were *The Count of Monte Cristo* and *The Three Musketeers*, was famous for his prodigious appetite for food and women. Mademoiselle Mars, a theatre diva, was a lover with whom he often dined, their meals commencing with Almond Soup.

It is said that Dumas' desire for this soup was sated only after a third serving, and this before he sampled the second course of turbot followed by pheasant or guinea-hen, partridge or quail, after which... 'Mademoiselle Mars has just enough time to slip into something more comfortable and I to unlace my boots surreptitiously for my feet always hurt me especially when I am at table.'[108]

---

108 Ekdah, Raviez Marilyn, *Erotic Cuisine, A Natural History of Aphrodisiac Cookery* Xlibrus

So in honour of his immense imagination and appetite for life, love, etc, there can be no better soup to sup...

All for one and one for all... Almond Soup[109]

Ingredients

Almonds - a quart (4 cups) pound skinned and blanched

Egg yolks - six (they must be hard boiled)

Chicken Stock - a quart (two pints)

Cream - a quart (two pints)

Method

Pound the almonds and hardboiled eggs yolks to a fine paste. Carefully mix together with the chicken stock and cream. Place over a gentle fire and stir well. Continue stirring to avoid the cream curdling then serve hot. (If this does not stir your amorous heart it may well stop it, considering all that cream!)

In 1778, a shipmate of explorer Captain James Cook wrote in his diary about a certain King La-

Corporation, 2000, p. 77

109 Douglas, Norman *Venus in the Kitchen* Bloomsbury, 2002 p. 11

petamaka II whom they had come across whilst visiting a Pacific Island. This king (apparently in his 80s) had endured, as one of his kingly duties, the task of deflowering every native maiden, a job that had to be carried out often up to ten times a day. Hence, he claimed never to have slept with the same woman twice. To maintain such vigour he recommended shrimp soup. So to all those lusty would-be kings out there, you will require:

King Lapetamaka's Lusty Shrimp Soup [110]
Ingredients

2 lbs of unshelled shrimp	Juice of a large lemon
1 small finely chopped pineapple	Juice of one fresh pineapple
1 cup of chicken broth	1 scallion
1 cup of sugar	3 tablespoons of molasses
½ a cup of vinegar	2 tablespoons of salt
6 cloves	2 tablespoons of corn starch
6 teaspoons allspice	1 tablespoon of ginger

Method
Rapidly boil 4 quarts of water, adding shrimp, scallion, allspice, salt cloves, lemon juice and cook for about ten minutes. Remove the shrimp, shelling and

---

110 Hendrickson, Robert *Lewd Food: The Complete Guide to Aphrodisiac Edibles* Chilton Book Company, 1974, p. 38

cleaning them. In a saucepan, simmer the chicken broth, molasses, ginger, vinegar and sugar. Separately blend the cornstarch and pineapple juice, adding into the pan and stirring the sauce frequently over a medium heat until it thickens. Finally, add the chopped pineapple and shrimp, heat for five minutes and serve.

Madame de Pompadour, mistress to Louis XV whom he dubbed his 'immaculate wonder', was tireless in her search for aphrodisiacs to excite the king. Amongst her most famous was celery soup, which she vowed was a passion inducer.

Madame P's 'immaculate & wonderful' Celery Soup

Ingredients

One stalk of Celery	Two egg yolks
Celery stock	One tablespoon of butter
1 small truffle	½ a cup of cream
A pinch of nutmeg	1 teaspoon of flour

Method

Chop celery, scald and drain, heat in a saucepan with a tablespoon of butter, add the flour, thickened stock and egg yolks mixed with cream, flavour with nutmeg and garnish with sliced truffles. But then anything with sliced truffles would have the, ahem, 'desired effect'.

'Encore un Moment...'

Madame Pompadour's successor and the last official mistress of King Louis XV was Madame Du Barry. Despite leading a most adventurous life, she lost her head during the terrors by the guillotine blade. Like her predecessor, she too dabbled in creative cookery to whet the appetite of her patron and is famed for her cauliflower soup – a dish you might lose your head over.

Soup du Barry Recipe [111]

Ingredients

1 small cauliflower, divided into small florets	1 egg yolk
6 cups chicken stock (or water)	1 large onion,
2 tbs white vinegar	chopped fine
Salt and freshly ground pepper	

[111] *Le Cordon Bleu at Home*, William Morrow Cookbooks 1991, p. 419-420

1 large leek (white part only, finely chopped)

1 cup crème fraiche or heavy cream

2 tablespoons unsalted butter

1/4 cup rice flour

Chervil or parley leaves for garnish

Method

Soak the cauliflower in cold water with the vinegar for five minutes. Sauté onion and leek in butter until soft. Add rice flour, stirring constantly for five minutes. Add in broth and cauliflower and cook until soft. Blend well. In separate bowl, mix egg yolk with cream. Add to soup mixture and press through food mill. Season with salt and pepper. Garnish with chervil or parsley.

Other dishes she is said to have inspired are soup of shrimps in chicken stock, spiced with dill; roast capon stuffed with puree of chestnuts and an omelette flavored with fresh ginger.

Bouillabaisse

This is a potent seafood soup. Legend has it that a lovelorn sailor sat on the Martiques Quay in Marseilles watching his beloved sail off in the arms of another, when she tossed him a liver of the racasse (or scorpion fish), by way of insult. Heart crushed, he did likewise with that liver, garlic and oil, then cooked it with pimento. Apparently, the flavours poured forth a scent so warming, his heartache instantly dissipated.

Another version of the story has it that the soup was conceived by Venus to prod Vulcan to new and more ardent amorous feats. According to another more Christian version, it was brought to the three Marys of the Gospel by angels.

These legends may have fishy origins, but as for the broth, it is served with a rust coloured peppery sauce (*rouillie*), topped with crusty freshly baked bread and sprinkled with cheese.

Isabelle Allende cites a Chilean version of the Bouillabaisse made with conger eel, described by the poet Pablo Neruda as thick and succulent – 'a boon to man.'

Finally to that stimulating aphrodisiac vegetable, fennel.

Sybaritic fennel soup[112]

Ingredients

1 large fennel bulb, trimmed and cut into small pieces, reserving fronds (leaves and stalks)

¾ cup dry white wine (sauvignon blanc)

One chicken bouillon cube (or 1 teaspoon chicken soup base)

½ cup cream

White pepper and salt

Method

Bring the wine to a boil in a saucepan, scrape in the fennel pieces and the chicken bouillon cube, lower heat, cover, and simmer till tender, about 10 minutes. Puree, solids first. If you want a very smooth soup, press through a sieve. Return to the saucepan, heat, and stir in the cream. Let simmer for a few minutes. Finely grind white pepper over the soup and stir in. Taste to see if it needs any salt. Ladle into two small bowls and serve hot to you and your honey, sprinkling finely minced fennel fronds over each right before you take to table.

---

112 http://www.soupsong.com/rfennel4.html

— Sweetmeats And Love Feasts —

Sitting comfortably?

Why, then the first rush of excitement has calmed! You have fallen out of lust and are slipping into love. This course has the capacity to be profound – where intimacy transcends the physical and evolves into something spiritual. (Although it can also stick in one's throat, lie heavy on one's stomach and/or create indigestion.)

Babette's Feast is a film about godly devotion and the sensuality of food. It is an adaptation of an Isak Dinesen short story, directed by Gabriel Axel and released in 1987. Babette has fled the 1870 revolution in Paris where she worked as a chef at the famous Café Anglais. She finds refuge in Jutland as a caretaker to two deeply pious Lutheran sisters and when finally the opportunity comes, Babette thanks them with a most sumptuous and exquisite meal. It is a meal only one of the diners (a retired army Captain) has ever experienced before.

A gourmet feast, it illustrates how a meal can unite both the physical and spiritual appetites and become a kind of love affair. Every dish served at this feast is a visual work of art and leaves the viewer salivating.

Babette's Feast

Potage a la Tortue
Real turtle soup accompanied by a bottle of
Amontillado sherry

§

Blinis Demidoff au Caviar
Caviar blinis served with a Veuve Cliquot 1860

§

Camille en Sarcophage avec Sauce Perigourdine
Tender, gamey quail stuffed with foie gras and
encased in a puff pastry shell, lies in a pool of black
Perigord truffles accompanied by a rare bottle of
Clos de Vougeot.
(This is Babette's piece-de résistance, which the
astonished Captain recognises as a famous dish
found only in the Café Anglais.)

§

La Salade

§

Les Fromages
Cheese and Fresh Fruit including highly exotic

fruits (to mid 19th century Jutland) such as pineapple, dates, papaya, grapes, candied fruits and angelica.

§

Baba au Rhum avec les Figues
Rum Cake with Dried Figs and an IIX Marc
fine champagne to end the evening

Flesh

Go along, go along quickly, and set all you have on the table for us. We don't want doughnuts, honey buns, poppy cakes, and other dainties; bring us a whole sheep, serve a goat and forty-year old mead! And plenty of vodka, not vodka with all sorts of fancies, not with raisins and flavorings, but pure foaming vodka, that hisses and bubbles like mad.

– Nikolai Gogol (1809-1852)

Some Meaty thoughts to chew upon

Through the ages many signature dishes have been dedicated to the patrons of famous chefs – Steak Chateaubriand, for example, is named after the Vicomte de Chateaubriand, whose voracious pursuit of pleasure both physical and edible continued unabated till his very last breath.

Beef Stroganoff was named after Russian diplomat Count Paul Stroganoff and Beef Wellington commemorates Napoleon's great adversary, Arthur Wellesley, the first Duke of Wellington.

Dishes have also been labelled after human body parts... Rabelais, that virtuoso of language, called the female pudendum a 'Mignon D'Amourette.' However, more conventionally, it refers to a cut of meat simply sautéed or grilled to keep the flesh on the inside a rosy pink colour. The 18th century actor and gastronome Denis Desenarts argued that 'A leg of lamb should be anticipated like the first meeting of lovers. Turks call it lady's thigh.'

Lady's Thighs

Ingredients

Kadin Budu Kofte	1 oz of flour
1 ½ lb of minced lamb	1 ½ teaspoons of salt
1 large onion	1 ½ teaspoons of black pepper
7 oz cooked rice	1 ½ teaspoons of ground cumin
45 ml grated white cheese	Oil for frying
1-2 beaten eggs	

Method

In a large bowl knead together all the ingredients until it forms a smooth paste. With dampened hands mould this paste into small balls, then gently flatten between your palms. Whilst heating oil in a large frying pan, dip the balls in beaten egg then fry turning occasionally. Your thighs when cooked should be golden in colour, dimpled and lush, remove and serve while still hot.[113]

Suggestive sausages

Brillat-Savarin author *The Physiology of Taste* recalled when 'At the table of a gentleman living in the Chausee D'antin... served up to his guest an Arles Sausage of an enormous size... 'It is really very large', said the lady casting on it a roguish glance, 'what a pity it is unlike anything I have ever seen...'

Fig-Fed Pork

– an ancient roman delicacy
The following is a succinct recipe belonging to one the earliest gourmets, Marcus Apicius, whereby a starved pig is crammed with dry figs

---

113 Lucan, Medlar, Gray, Durian *The Decadent Cookbook* Dedalus, 2009, p. 172

and then given mead to drink. The ingredients react with one another: the figs expand in the stomach due to the mead. This causes the pig acute indigestion, the enlargement of its liver, and eventual death.

Fig fed pork liver (that is liver crammed with figs) is prepared in a wine sauce with a pepper, thyme, lovage broth, a little wine and oil.

If the above isn't quite the sort of dish you had in mind you might prefer this...

Suckling Pig with Eels

This dish requires a young suckling pig, no more than fifteen days old and enough eel meat to fill the pig's intestines. The eel meat should be boned and washed in vinegar before being stuffed into the intestinal tubes and seasoned with peppercorns, cloves and plenty of sage. The suckling, with refilled intestines is then roasted. Norman Douglas, cele-brated aphrodisical epicurean highly recommends this dish, describing it as extremely appetising and stimulating.[114]

114 Douglas, Norman *Venus in the Kitchen* Bloomsbury, 2002, p. 138

Shall we proceed, in time at least... From stuffed intestines to testicles!

Scappi's Blessed Balls

Bartolomeo Scappi was the head chef to two Popes during the Renaissance. His book *Opera dell'arte del cucinare* published in 1570 was a bestseller with numerous reprints. Containing more than a 1000 recipes, it covered all aspects of cookery, from how to pick the best young suckling pig or set up a spit in a field, to how to prepare a peacock sauce with toasted almonds.

Scappi's Balls-Recipe 50 [115]

'To prepare a dainty pottage of the testicles of a lamb or a suckling calf, get the testicles just as soon as the animal is killed: cut away the scrotum and still raw, cut them crosswise into slices. Put those into a small saucepan or pot containing melted chicken fat that is not too hot, sauté them, slowly stirring them. When they have shrunk and firmed up, add in a little chicken or veal broth that is not too salty, a little cinnamon and saffron and boil that. Then put in the

---

115 Scully Terence, *The Opera of Bartolomeo Scappi (1570): The Art and Craft of a Master Cook* University of Toronto Press; 2008, p. 558

ingredients used in the previous recipe, (gooseber-
ries peeled, seeded, and verjuice grapes, along with
a little beaten fine herb). It's optional whether you
thicken the broth with beaten fresh eggs. You can
do the udder of a suckling calf the same way.'

To add a certain hop to your step you might like
a recipe given by Norman Douglas in his 1952
Venus in the Kitchen...

Hare Croquettes [116]

Ingredients

Minced roast hare	Eggs
A small onion	Breadcrumbs
Salt and Pepper	Parmesan Cheese
Mixed Ground Spice	Garlic and Ginger to taste

Method
Bind together the ingredients, divide out the mixture in small croquettes and fry.

---

116 Douglas, Norman *Venus in the Kitchen* Bloomsbury, 2002, p. 107

For Latin Lovers, a sprinkling of Machismo from the Futurists.

Ultra virile

On a rectangular plate put some thin slices of **calf's tongue** boiled and cut lengthwise, on top of these arrange lengthwise along the axis of the plate two parallel rows of **spit-roasted prawns**. Between these two rows place the body of a **lobster** previously boned and shelled. Cover in **zabaglione**. At the tail end of the lobster place three halves of **hard boiled eggs**, to be cut lengthwise so that the yellows rest on the slices of tongue. The front part, however, is crowned with **six cockscombs** (the cap of a rooster) laid out like sectors of a circle, while completing the garnish are two rows of little cylinders composed of a little wheel of **lemon**, slices of **grape** and slices of **truffle**, sprinkled with **lobster coral**.[117]

The following recipe comes from a chance discovery – *Fanny Hill's Cook Book*. This is a book completely of its time (the 1970s so prepare

---

[117] Tommaso Marinetti (translated by Suzanne Brill) *The Futurist Cookbook* Trefoil Publications Ltd 1989, p. 558

yourselves), with the sauciest of illustrations and funniest recipes. It is terribly un-PC and among the many *double entendres* recipes in the book one will find such gems as French Freud Potatoes, Devils' Drip (for gravy), Sexpot aufeu, etc. It really shouldn't work but it is an absolute hoot and jaw dropper.

Cunnilinguini With Pietro's Tongue [118]

'Here's how Pietro does cunnilinguini. First, he calls up Theresa and if she feels like coming, she brings over her cunnilinguini and washes it off thoroughly. Then Pietro gets her cunnilinguini hot and moist and throws in his tongue. However, between the first act and last emission there are a few agile twists to the plot particularly if you want to eat with Theresa and have her, too.'

Ingredients

1lb linguini

Pinch of white pepper

Three eggs

Three tbs butter

1 cup grated Parmesan Cheese

Pinch salt

½ lb cooked smoked beef tongue cut into ½ inch slices

118 Braun Lional H. & Adams William *Fanny Hill's Cook Book* Taplinger Publishing, 1971, p. 81

Method

Bring salted water to a fast boil and add linguini cooking for 7 minutes, *al dente*. Prepare sauce while pasta is cooking. Cut tongue into bite sized cubes. Beat eggs adding pinch of salt and pepper.
Drain her linguini off in colander and replace in hot pot. Add your eggs, cheese and stick in your tongue and mix thoroughly with linguine. Be certain her linguini is hot enough to allow your eggs to be gently cooked by her linguini heat. Then butter her linguini and cook entire mixture over a very low flame for 1-½ minutes. Serve at once. Remember when Theresa's cunnilinguini is drained and eaten and Pietro's tongue has completely disappeared they've both come to certain conclusions... *It's not how long you make it, it's how long you make it last!* Therefore, eat slowly but carry a big stick.

For a very 'Big Night'

Big Night is a foodie film extraordinaire, directed by Campbell Scott and Stanley Tucci, released in 1996. Set in the 1950s, it is the story of two immigrant Italian brothers, Primo and Secondo who are desperate to make their gourmet Italian restaurant a success. However, the locals want only what they are used to, Italian-American meat-balls and spaghetti, so most nights their restaurant is empty. As a last resort Secondo's friend Pascal, promises to get the famous singer Louis Prima to eat at the restaurant, in the hope the celebrity's dining there will put it on the map. The brothers invest all they have in the anticipated 'big night'.

The showpiece of the meal is a dish called Timpani, which is a 'drum' filled with layers of pasta, meat, sauce and eggs that looks like a large cake. The preparation of the timpani is beautifully filmed such that the screen positively exudes the dish. The brothers are almost in awe of their finished creation, treating it as a work of art. With much expectation, they serve their invited guests and anxiously await a reaction. Finally, it comes in the words of Louis Prima: 'God damn it this is so fucking good I should kill you.'

Big Night Timpani for a feast

The Dough

4 cups all-purpose flour

4 large eggs

1 teaspoon salt

3 tablespoons olive oil

1/2 cup water

Butter and Olive Oil to prepare the pan

The Filling

2 cups 1/4 x 1/2-inch Genoa salami pieces (approx. 3/4 lb.)

2 cups 1/4 x 1/2-inch sharp provolone cheese pieces (approx. 3/4 lb.)

12 hard-boiled eggs, shelled, quartered lengthwise and then each quarter cut in half

to create chunks

2 cups little meatballs about 1 diameter

8 cups Sunday Sauce following the note at the beginning of recipe

3 pounds, ziti or penne, cooked very al dente (about half the time recommended on

the package) and drained (18 cups cooked)

2/3 cup finely grated pecorino Romano cheese

4 large eggs, beaten

If the above proves too heavy a dish one might prefer to tip the scales of love in a more briny direction.

> *... some foods are for lovers, some for philosophers and some for tax collectors. A lad has a girl he is courting... I place before him cuttle-fishes, squids and various rock fishes served with dainty sauces... for a person like that... has his thoughts continually on love-making.*
>
> – The Deipnosophists in Book IX, Athenaeus

Fantastically fishy, this recipe allows for no half measures and is dedicated to the more extravagant amongst us.

Salmon à la Rothschild[119]

A sumptuous dish consisting of the most lavish ingredients, a large salmon soaked in no less than four bottles of champagne, stuffed to the gills with mussels, smelts and crayfish tails, then covered in truffle shavings.

Ingredients

1 enormous salmon	24 smelts
4 bottles champagne	4 whiting
1lbs truffles pared and sliced	1 large loaf stale French bread
20 small crayfish	2 pints of stock
1lb steamed mussels	6 ounces butter
5 small soles	1 tablespoon thick béchamel sauce
3 egg yolks	1 egg white
6 ounces best mirepoix	Chervil, parsley, tarragon
Salt, pepper, nutmeg	Tarragon vinegar

For the stuffing and paste: four whiting – poached lightly

119 Kelly, Ian Cooking for Kings: The Life of the First Celebrity Chef Antonin Careme Short Books Ltd, 2004, p. 247

Method

Create a 'panada' by soaking the bread in fish stock and after an hour squeeze out the excess moisture. Add to this the butter and flaked cooked whiting and a tablespoon of thick béchamel sauce, three egg yolks, two tablespoons of fine herbs, (a mixture of chervil, parsley and tarragon), a little nutmeg and pound thoroughly. Then pass the mixture through a sieve and set aside.

Next, stuff the salmon with the mixture, then sew it up. A layer of the remaining mixture is applied to the salmon as an extra skin, to which truffle scales are painstakingly applied. Place the salmon in a fish kettle with a mirepoix (a sieved mixture of carrots, onions and celery), then soak the salmon in four bottles of champagne and bring to the boil. Once the liquid has boiled, cover the fish in a buttered paper, place in a medium oven and cook for two hours. Finally when it is ready serve the salmon on a large dish with a ragout of escallops of fillets of sole à la vénitienne, steamed crayfish tails, mussels and eights hatelets (skewers) composed of fried smelts. Accompany this piscine extravagance with the champagne sauce strained in boats.

Now, a most slippery aphrodisiac.

Baked Eels
Norman Douglas gives us a lush casserole recipe involving eel, butter, grated nutmeg, salt, parsley, mushrooms, white wine and French brandy, slowly cooked on a medium fire. 'Nothing,' he 'wrote, can be better – for those who like eels.'[120]

Lobster
There are so many ways to cook this kingly crustacean; one may be partial to Plain Lobster, Chinese Garlic Lobster, and Lobster with Whiskey, Creamy Lobster Bisque, Lobster Thermidor, Lobster à la Portos, Lobster Amandine.

> A woman should never be seen eating or drinking, unless it be lobster, salad and champagne. The only true feminine and becoming viands.
> – Lord Byron

Indeed, lobster may well be a dish most appreciated by the ladies – and an artist most appreciative of womankind was the brilliantly bohemian and wonderfully eccentric Toulouse-Lautrec whose cookbook The Art of Cuisine includes...

120 Douglas, Norman Venus in the Kitchen Bloomsbury, 2002, p. 28

Lobster Americaine

Ingredients

3-4 tbs oil   ¼ cup of wine
½ cup of cognac   ¾ tomato sauce
¾ meat glaze

This sauce is useful for simmering extra lobster meat. Also, add shells, cracked for flavour. Sieve sauce. Bind with 1 tbs butter for each cup of reduced sauce.

This recipe can be varied for different shellfish - shrimp, crayfish or small frozen South African lobster tails.

Let us meander forth. Norman Douglas in *Venus in the Kitchen* dishes up a succinct snail recipe very much like Apicius', which he dedicates to a friend hence the title.

Snails à la cc

This dish requires patience, diligence and time.
Take your **snails** and place them in an earthen
container. Daily, for the next two weeks feed your
snails **a glass of milk**. On the eve of one's intended
seduction, soak the snails overnight in an infusion
of **water**, **vinegar** and **salt**.
Once ready to cook, make sure they are washed and
then boiled. Next, they are pulled from their shells,
dipped in **beaten eggs** and fried in **olive oil**. Serve
with a piquant **fish sauce**; Douglas recommends
elaeologarum, a mixture of lovage, coriander, and
rue oil and fish stock.

Fowl... Play!

*What is sauce for the goose may be sauce for the gander, but
it is not necessarily sauce for chicken, the duck, the turkey or
the guinea hen.*

– Alice B. Toklas

A French Love Recipe[121]

(For those partial to all manner of poultry)

One large olive - stuffed with paste of anchovy capers and oil

Put inside a trussed and boned Garden Warbler

Put inside a fat ottoman

Put inside a boned lark

Put inside a boned thrush

Put inside a fat quail then wrap in vine leaves

Put inside a boned lapwing

Put inside a boned golden plover

Put inside a red legged Partridge

Put inside a boned woodcock then roll in breadcrumbs

Put inside a boned teal

Put inside a boned guinea fowl

Put inside a larded duck

Put inside a fat fowl

Put inside a well hung pheasant

Put inside a fat wild goose

Put inside a fine turkey

Put inside a boned bustard

---

121 Hendrickson, Robert *Lewd Food: The Complete Guide to Aphrodisiac Edibles* Chilton Book
Company, 1974, p. 153

Place in a saucepan with onions, cloves, carrots, ham, celery, mignonette, and bacon garlic, pepper and salt. Close the saucepan with pastry and cook gently.

On how to make chicken tender

Toulouse-Lautrec advises the following method – not one I have personally tested, so we will have to take his word for it.

In order to make chickens immediately edible, take them out of the hen run, pursue them into open county and when you have made them run, kill them with a gun loaded with very small shot.

The meat of the chicken gripped with fright will become tender. This method used in the country of the Fangs (Gabon) seems infallible even for the oldest and toughest hens.

Chicken with almonds[122] – Lautrec

Ingredients

Two broilers sautéed with three onions in three tbs butter

122 Toulouse- Lautrec & Joyant, M *The Art of Cuisine* Holt Rinehart Winston, 1966, p. 112

For simmering, add 2 tbs each white wine and cognac, ½ cup of bouillon

¼ lb of cubed ham

2 tbs bacon cubes

1 tbs flour for sauce

1 ½ cups of heavy cream

Take some nice chicken and cut them in pieces without break-
ing the bones. In a heavy and shallow straight-sided sauce-
pan, brown some cut onions, a dash of garlic and shallot then
the pieces of chicken so that they are a good golden colour.
This done pour the contents of the pan into a big saucepan,
having strained the liquid so that the garlic and onion are
removed. Put in the pieces of chicken and add butter, a finger
of wine and of cognac, a bouquet garni, cloves, pepper, salt,
– just moisten with bouillon. Add the chopped livers, pieces
of ham cut fine and cubes of raw bacon. Sprinkle with a little
flour. Let it reduce and simmer until there is no liquid.
Just before you serve, make a sauce with four to six egg yolks
to which cream has been added and bind over a gentle fire or
in a double boiler so that the sauce does not curdle. Add the
juice of one lemon and in the sauce mix well some almonds
and hazelnuts pounded into small pieces Arrange pieces of
chicken at the bottom of a warm dish, cover it all with sauce
and garnish the dish with croutons, well sautéed in butter.

For a more eastern flavour:

Zahra Palau

This pilaf dish for the main course comes from Afghanistan, delicious and sensuous...

Ingredients

25g/1oz-blanched almonds	125ml/4fl oz light chicken stock or water
25g/1oz pistachio nuts	2 tablespoons granulated sugar
2 tablespoons oil or ghee	3 tablespoons water grated rind of one orange
1 small onion, finely chopped	100g/4oz long grain rice
Two chicken breasts, quartered	1 teaspoon saffron

Method

Fry the onions and pistachios in the oil or ghee and set them aside. Fry the onion lightly and set aside. Fry the chicken until golden, add the saffron and the stock and simmer for 20 minutes or until tender. While the chicken is cooking, cook the rice in plenty of boiling, salted water. When just tender, drain and keep warm. Dissolve the sugar in the water, add the orange peel and boil to make thick syrup. Arrange the chicken pieces on top of the rice with the onion, and nuts, add the chicken liquid and finally pour the syrup over.

Finally, should that not sufficiently arouse you, it is worth mentioning that the following dish is from Arabian *Book of the Thousand Nights and One Night*.[123] A dish certainly fit to inflame a kingly passion.

He took two ounces of Chinese cubebs; one ounce of fat extract of Ionian hemp; one ounce of fresh caryophyle (pinks); one ounce of red cinnamon from Serendib, then drachms of white Malabar cardamom, five of Indian ginger, five of white pepper, five of pimento from the isles, one ounce of the berries of Indian star anise, and half an ounce of mountain thyme. These he mixed cunningly, after having pounded and sieved them. He added pure honey until the whole became a thick paste: then he mingled five grains of musk and an ounce of pounded fish roe with the rest. Finally he added a little concentrated rose water and put all in the bowl saying ...
Here is a sovereign mixture which will harden the eggs and thicken the sap when it becomes too thin. You must eat this paste two hours before the sexual approach, but for three days before that you must eat nothing save roast pigeons excessively seasoned with spice, male fish with the cream complete and lightly friend rams eggs. If after all that you do not pierce the very walls of the room and then get the founda-

123 Mather Joseph Charles, Mardrus E.P *Book of the Thousand Nights and One Night* Routledge and Kegan Paul plc 1986, p. 96

tions of the house with child you can cut off my beard and spit in my face.

Should none of the above work, one could always try something more hardcore. A US love charm for old maids instructs them to kill an 11 month old game rooster and before the body cools extract the heart, swallow whole raw and if you don't choke you will be married in 11 months.[124]

For those who do not relish the ingestion of flesh, abundant mother earth provides a veritable A-Z of vegetables to play with, starting with Artichokes and continuing all the way to Zucchini. However, for our explicit purposes 'T' seems a teasing, tantalising letter to tarry at...

Truffles

When not supping soup with Mademoiselle Mars, Dumas dined with Mademoiselle George a famous actress of the Odeon Theatre. These evenings were dedicated to truffles, specifically a truffle salad. In his memoirs, Dumas noted some of Mademoiselle George's dishes were

---

124 Hendrickson, Robert *Lewd Food: The Complete Guide to Aphrodisiac Edibles* Chilton Book Company, 1974, p. 149

'like incendiary fireboats', with an added suggestive comment that 'She (George) had a very
different knowledge from Mademoiselle Mars.'

'On her dining table [rested] a huge gold
and silver bowl filled to overflowing with 5 or
6 pounds of truffles whose priceless scent perfumed the air... Mademoiselle George peeled
these with a silver knife and seasoned them with
champagne, almond milk or another liqueur as
her mood suited. Other prepared aspics, pates
and dishes were served from the kitchen and carried into the dining room by guests. (Then came
the famous salade, marking the beginning of the
evening's pleasures...).' [125]

Truffles [126]

Par boil the **truffles**, sprinkle with **salt** and fasten
them on skewers, half fry them, then place them in a
sauce pan with **oil, broth, virgin olive oil, reduced
wine, pepper** and **honey**; allow them to finish. Bind
the liquor with roux, prick the truffles so they may
become saturated with the juice, dress them nicely,
and when really hot, serve.

125 Ekdah, Raviez Marilyn, *Erotic Cuisine, A Natural History of Aphrodisiac Cookery*, Xlibrus
Corporation, 2000, p. 78
126 Apicius (translated by Joseph Dommers Vehling) *Cooking and Dining in Imperial Rome*,
[EBook #29728] p. 315

Truffles — anyone who does not declare himself ready to leave Paradise or Hell for such a treat is not worthy to be born again.

— Maurice Goudeket, *Close to Colette*

The truffle is a virtuoso of adaptability and can be added to almost any dish: pasta, risotto, meats, fish, salads, omelettes. They can be inlaid in goose livers, turkey breasts, fish, oysters or served in a white napkin and eaten with shavings of butter. For the more sweet-toothed, they can be found in fondues, chocolates, even ice cream (a popular 19th century flavour still served today).

Madame de Pompadour used truffles to 'heat the blood'. It is said she followed a strict aphrodisiac regime — a diet of vanilla, truffles and celery — as she complained that continual love-making exhausted her. Her 'Filet de Sole Pompadour' with forcemeat of truffle was a dish much appreciated by Louis XV. Such was this pair's dedication to the pleasure of dining à deux, they installed a mechanized table in the room where they ate. This table could descend through an opening in the floor, for privacy, to the level below and be reset for the next course. Her successor Madame du Barry followed Pompadour's example and used truffle sweetbreads to arouse.

— A Bit On The Side —

The following chapter pays homage to the courtesans and demimondaines who were responsible throughout the ages for creating many edible and aphrodisiacal delights; after all, the responsibility of maintaining, sustaining and increasing their patrons' libidos fell within the job remit.

Known as the *well beloved*, the French king Louis XV (as I have mentioned before in these pages), had his palate famously pampered by his mistresses, Madame Pompadour and the Comtesse du Barry. Both women left their mark on French cooking. By the same token it seems some chefs of royalty were expected to tend to all manner of their kings' appetites... as evidenced by Pierre La Varenne, famed chef and author of *La Cuisine Francais*, (1651) who selected ladies to introduce to Henri IV.

Public dining in restaurants, as we understand it, originated in France during the 18th century partly as a result of the French revolution when surplus chefs (who had lost their aristocratic patrons), decided to open their own establish-ments.

Houses of ill repute and moral turpitude also contributed to the rise in restaurants, catering to the tastes of their clientele by serving all manner of tid-bits. The reverse was also true with many restaurants catering to their customers' needs by providing private rooms. [127]

Most famous was Laperouse in the 6th arron-dissement of Paris, which provided 'petits sa-lons', guaranteeing their clients discretion. In-deed, a clause in French law made any accusa-tion of adultery invalid if the reported incident occurred in a public place, which was just what these 'petits salons' were considered to be. One needed to prove that adultery had taken place in private in order to make the charge stick.

[127] The first true restaurant proprietor is believed to have been Monsieur A.Boulanger; a soup vendor, who in 1765 opened his business on the Rue Bailleul, in Paris. The sign above his door advertised restoratives. Members of the guilds saw it as an infringement on their business and declared Boulanger was making a 'ragout' or stew which the 'Guild de Traiteurs' had the only legal right to produce. Boulanger's establishment was shut down and he ended up in court but won his case. By 1804 Paris had more than 500 restaurants.

Most illustrious of all Nineteenth century Paris restaurants was probably the Café Anglais. On June 7, 1867, the Café Anglais served the now-famous 'Three Emperors Dinner' for three royal guests visiting Paris to attend the Universal Exposition. The diners included Tsar Alexander II of Russia, his son the Tsarevich (later the tsar Alexander III) and King William I of Prussia, later the first emperor of Germany. http://www.tallyrand. info/historychefs/restaurant-history.shtml

Senators, politicians and captains of industry met their waiting courtesans via a hidden stairway. Later, during the Belle Époque, Laperouse became a favourite meeting spot for a more bohemian crowd: Guy de Maupassant, Émile Zola, Colette and Alexandre Dumas fils were all regulars.

The Tasting Menu

When I began writing this chapter I could have listed any number of vegetable concoctions – creamed spinach, a sizzling aubergine dish or Chartreuse carrots glazed in fresh Swiss Alpine butter. But the following menus seemed to me far more provocative.

Thus, in honour of those courtesans, I include – unconventionally perhaps – a selection of 'side orders' courtesy of an 18th century best-seller entitled *Harris's List of Covent Garden Ladies*, an annual guide detailing the names and specialties of London's prostitutes – an essential guide for any epicurean gentleman in pursuit of pleasure. Hundreds of women were listed and the book was updated annually. The following is an assortment of what one may (or may not) look forward to:

From the annual dated 1764 we have **Mrs. Bland** of Wardour Street, described as a gay volatile girl, who 'makes use of provocatives; such as pigs, veal, new laid eggs, oysters, crabs, prawns and eryngoes...' Harris notes 'her appetite is insatiable and goes on to say that 'sometimes (she) leaves the marks of her penetrating teeth on her paramours cheeks.' [128]

However a dish to avoid at all costs was...
Bet Ellis
This poor lady is described as a diminutive, smirking, lecherous hussy: 'a very wart upon the crudities of Venus.' Harris further demeans her, 'neither her teeth nor her legs are good, and being red haired she emits a unsavory effluvia which alone is enough to damp the ardor of an elegant debauchee.' (Annual of 1761)[129]

Mrs Hamblin, we are told, had been in the business for 30 years and was most adept at servicing the more elderly gent. At the other end of the spectrum was the enchanting and wanton nymph at No. 44 Mortimer Street, Cavendish Square, described as having 'panting orbs, pout-

---

128 Rubenhold, Hallie *Harris's List of Covent Garden Ladies* Tempus, 2005 p. 155
129 Ibid., p. 136-137

ing lips, delicate shape and love sparkling eyes'. Harris fairly rhapsodizes about this girl and describes her as an offspring of delight, of only 18 summers, which the reader 'for a compliment of five guineas (may) be in full possession of.'

Also found within the pages of this curious and comprehensive list is **Miss Lawrence** of No. 6 Church Street, St. Ann, Soho, described as a young Israelite who renounced her Levetical friends for the sake of a Christian and will now open her synagogue of love even on the Sabbath to Jew, Turk or infidel!

And continuing in the same fashion,

Warning Adult Content Follows...
A renowned London lothario sent the following to me – his own epicurean revelling in the female form, alas, cut short by marriage. It is the 1912 menu from an American brothel; easily found on the internet, it may not be to the taste of the faint hearted or morally fastidious, but I for one was rapt. It may be a fake (note the name of the madam!), but it's fascinating all the same...

'Mrs. F. A. Tasse having opened a Rapacious Capsulation Parlor at Twenty Second Street requests ... patronage of the fast slow and smart set.'

Menu

French fashion with finger in ass hole
$3.50

Common old-fashioned fuck
$2.50

Diddling on the edge of the bed, with one foot on the floor
$2

Fucking the breast with tits tight
$1

Blowing in the ass hole, new style
$1.70

Finger fucking with juice
50 cents

Dog Fashion
$2.80

Dry bob
49 cents

Sitting on prick shoving in stones and all
$2.59

One female suck off stones in mouth

$2.59

One fuck ten minutes soaks

$2.65

Pinky Special

Under fucking woman on top tits in your face with extra lady to play with your balls while blowing wind up your ass hole with goose quill

$30.00

Ass hole fucking for men over 45

$1

Bob cocks and flat pricks extra

50 cents

'No discount for cash. Stink fingers and jerk off matinees for young men under 21, every Wednesday from 2.30 p.m. to 4 p.m. customer must enter with cash in one had and tool in the other. If you are not a self-starter stay at home and jack yourself off.'

— Happy Ever Afters —

There is, undoubtedly, a universal desire for the sweet things in life. Hailing from every corner of this globe come the most delicious offerings: Chinese love-cakes made of Wisteria blossoms, exquisitely executed petit fours originally made for Louis XIV in tiny ovens, Baba au Rhum created by Poland's dethroned King Stanislaw II and Persian sherbet as mentioned in the Asian love manual the *Ananga Ranga* – it is said that no Persian will drink sherbet in the presence of his mother-in-law! – to the English lush's luscious sherry-soaked 'tipsy cake' or trifle.

One's heart may dance at the mention of Peach Melba or Pavlova (the former so-called because Dame Nellie Melba, the legendary soprano, lent her name to the dish after it was thrown together by Georges Escoffer in a moment of passion following the singer's delectable performance in Wagner's *Lohengrin*). Pavlova, meanwhile, was created by an enterprising chef in Western Australia during the 1930s in honour of the ballerina Anna Pavlova, who looked picture-perfect in her creamy, meringue-like tutu.

There are soufflés, mousses, jellies and blancmange, the latter a white sweet pudding made from almond milk, gelatine and flavoured with rum. In the French film *La Grand Bouffe* one of the lead characters dies face-down in a pair of blancmange breasts after participating in the orgy to end all orgies.

Frangipani, the pastry cake filled with cream sugar and almonds, is said by some to have been invented by the Marquis Frangipani, a pleasure-loving general under Louis XIV. However the Italians have it that frangipani was borne of the love Count Cesare Frangipani had for Catherine di Medici. As for Marzipan, Raymond Oliver wrote in his *Gastronomy of France*:

'It must be light. I have already explained that we are dealing with the problem of restoring forces or of preparing for exertions (of the most splendid order).'

One could rhapsodise eternally about chocolates, chocolate desserts, dense puddings, mille feuille, cakes, gateaux, candied fruits, liqueur-soaked sponges, fruits, tarts, pies, creams, flaming crêpes...

But the adage 'a moment on the lips, a lifetime on the hips' does, regrettably, contain an ounce of truth. No matter – on we go to...

The Crème de la Crème, Carème's Creams

'The fine arts are five in number: painting, sculpture, poetry, music, architecture – whose main branch is confectionary.'

Antoine Carème (1784-1833) is regarded as the inventor of haute cuisine and the world's first celebrity chef. He cooked for every European sovereign worthy of their crown. He made Napoleon's wedding cake, soufflés flecked with gold for the Rothschilds in Paris, and meals for the Romanovs in Russia.

One of his famous desserts was his patisserie *gross meringue à la Parisienne*, meringues flavoured with Seville orange peel and crème fouetté.

Amongst his inventions were Charlotte Russes and Apple Charlotte. His creations were so valued that it's said they were stolen from the table at the court of George IV, not to be relished at home but sold on at hugely inflated prices.

Crème fouetté au Marasquin[130]

Place a quart of **double cream** in a bowl and leave in a basin of ice for two hours allowing it to set. Add a pinch of **gum tragacanth** in powder and then whisk

---

130 Lucan, Medlar, Gray, Durian *The Decadent Cookbook* Dedalus, 2009, p. 190

for fifteen minutes till light and stiff. Next, stir in six ounces of **pounded sugar**. Prior to serving, add **Marasquin** (cherry liqueur) then pour the cream in a crust of tart paste, sweet vol-au-vent or almond paste cups.

Crème Fouette à la Rose

Prepare as above. Once beaten, add a half a spoonful of **essence of roses**, six ounces of **pounded sugar** and **red food colouring** (an infusion of cochineal, carmine, or *rouge vegetal*). However, if served white (without food colouring) some **strawberries** may be placed upon it.[131]

We shall dilly-dally a while in Paris with sweet Amélie Poulain who entered into our consciousness in the romantic comedy *Amélie* in 2001, a film directed by Jean-Pierre Jeunet.

Amélie is the beautiful dreamer, too comfortable in her own imagination to meet reality. A waitress at the café The Two Windmills, she tries her best to better the lives of her quirky customers. Amélie derives pleasure from wearing raspberries on her fingers like thimbles, plung-

---

131 Lucan, Medlar, Gray, Durian *The Decadent Cookbook* Dedalus, 2009, p. 191

ing her hand into a cool sack of grain and most famously the ritual were she has to crack open the brittle, caramelized top of an ice-cold crème Brûlée.

Amélie's Crème Brûlée[132]

Ingredients

2 ½ cups heavy cream

4 large egg yolks, well beaten

¼ to 1/3 cup superfine sugar

Method

Boil the cream for about 30 seconds then pour into the beaten egg yolks, and whisk them together. Return the mixture to the pan and stir under a low heat until the mixture thickens and coats the spoon. Pour into a shallow baking dish. Refrigerate overnight. Before serving sprinkle an even layer of sugar upon the chilled cream then place it under a grill preheated to the maximum temperature (or use a blowtorch). The sugar will caramelize to a sheet of brown smoothness.

132 This is an old crème brûlée recipe that dates back to 1909. It was taken from *The Ocklye Cookery Book* by Eleanor L. Jenkinson. [via GourmetSleuth]

Scrumptious! However, before we get too whimsical...

Chocolate Salty Balls

'Chocolate Salty Balls' is a 1998 song recipe from the animated comedy TV series *South Park*, performed by the character Chef (the late Isaac Hayes). The song reached No.1 on the UK and Irish Singles Chart.

Chef's ingredients are listed in the first and second verses. Curiously however, there is no mention of salt in the recipe. Directions are also given as to how they should be eaten, i.e. sucked rather than chewed, and he advocates their aphrodisiacal properties: 'Say, everybody, have you seen my balls/they're big and salty and brown/ if you ever need a quick pick-me-up/just stick my balls in your mouth'.

Sadly, by the final verse it appears that his hot chocolate salty balls have inadvertently been burned, and so urges his lover to blow on them.

Chef's Chocolate Salty Balls[133]

Ingredients

Two tablespoons of cinnamon

Two or three egg whites

A half a stick of butter, melted

Quarter cup of unsweetened chocolate

Half a cup of brandy

Bag or two of sugar

A pinch of vanilla

The above may be considered a little too risqué or juvenile for some – but surely not as naughty as Ms.Toklas' Hashish Brownies...

The Alice B. Toklas Cookbook, first published in 1954, is one of America's great works of recollection, culinary or otherwise. Toklas lived with her companion the writer Gertrude Stein, the pair being firm fixtures of the Parisian avant-garde. Amongst the 300 recipes in her book are dishes such as Stuffed Artichokes Stravinsky, Gigot de la Clique, and Bavarian Cream Perfect Love. However, it was Toklas' fudge that caused a stir.

Apparently it was the artist Brion Gysin who came up with a recipe known as 'The Food of Paradise':

---

133 'Chocolate Salty Balls' lyrics on http://www.metrolyrics.com

'it might provide an entertaining refreshment for a Ladies' Bridge Club or a chapter meeting of the Daughters of the American Revolution. In Morocco it is thought to be good for warding off the common cold in damp winter weather and is, indeed, more effective if taken with quantities of hot mint tea. Euphoria and brilliant storms of laughter; ecstatic reveries and extensions of one's personality on several simultaneous planes are to be complacently expected. Almost anything Saint Theresa did, you can do better if you can bear to be ravished by 'un evanouisement reveille'(an evocative swoon).'

Alice B. Toklas's Hashish Fudge

Ingredients

1 teaspoon black peppercorns, one whole nutmeg, four average sticks of cinnamon, 1 teaspoon of coriander, a bunch of Cannabis sativa: these should all be pulverised in a mortar.

About a handful each of stoned dates, dried figs, shelled almonds and peanuts: chop these and mix them together.

Method

The cannabis, along with the spices, should be dusted over the mixed fruit and nuts, then kneaded together. Dissolve about a cup of sugar in a big pat of butter. Rolled into a cake and cut into pieces or made into balls about the size of a walnut, it should be eaten with care. *Two pieces are quite sufficient.*

'Obtaining the cannabis may present certain difficulties... It should be picked and dried as soon as it has gone to seed and while the plant is still green.'

A more oriental version may be something along the lines of the following:

Majoon
'This dessert will make all women want to cast off their clothes and run naked through the streets!' [134]

Ingredients

7 g cannabis buds

1 cup chopped dates

½ cup honey

½ cup chopped raisins or currants

1 teaspoon each ground nutmeg, anise seed and ginger

½ cup ground walnuts

½ cup water

2 tablespoons melted butter

---

134 Hendrickson, Robert *Lewd Food: The Complete Guide to Aphrodisiac Edibles* Chilton Book Company, 1974, p. 308

Method

In an ungreased skillet, toast cannabis over low heat until golden brown, taking care not to scorch it. Transfer to a food processor and add dates, honey, raisins, walnuts, anise seed, nutmeg and ginger. Process to a lumpy paste. Transfer mixture to a medium saucepan, add water and cook over low heat until ingredients have softened and are well blended. While the mixture is hot, add the melted butter and stir for 5 minutes. Allow mixture to cool, then seal in a glass jar and keep under refrigeration. Majoon can be spread on crackers or bread, or used as a pastry filling.

Time I think to inject some family-friendly desserts... What could be more wholesome than **American Apple Pie**. Although, perhaps not, if you have seen the movie of a similar name!

All-American Apple Pie

Ingredients

Pie dough for a double crust, chilled

4 pounds (about 6 very large) apples

¼ teaspoon salt

2 tablespoons graham cracker crumbs (or dry bread crumbs)

¾ cup of sugar	2 tablespoons quick cooking tapioca
Grated zest of one lemon	1/8 - ¼ teaspoon freshly grated nutmeg
½ teaspoon ground cinnamon	

2 tablespoons cold unsalted butter cut into bits

For the glaze (optional): Milk or heavy cream

Decorating: coarse or granulated sugar

Method

An excruciatingly laborious, protracted and tedious method for making the pie can be found in the source material and should you wish to try the recipe I am certain you will be well rewarded.[135]

For something simpler, let us turn to Mrs Beeton and her apple snowballs.

Apple Snowballs

An alternative, perhaps, to chocolate salty balls?

Ingredients

Two teacupfuls of rice   Apples

---

135 Greenspan, Dorie Baking from My home to yours Houghton Mifflin Harcourt, 2006 p. 300-302

Milk   Moist sugar

Cloves

Method

Boil the rice in milk separately until three-parts
done, then strain it off, and pare and core the apples
without dividing them. Put a small quantity of sugar
and a clove into each apple, put the rice round them,
and tie each ball separately in a cloth. Boil until the
apples are tender (about 1/2 to 1 hour); then take
them up, remove the cloths, and serve.

This dish is in season from August to March.[136]

And for those who seek poetical lyricism with
their sweet deliciousness, I recommend *Tart-
elettes Amandines* by Edmond Rostand from *Cyrano
de Bergerac*, Act II, Scene IV (1898).

Tartelettes Amandine

Ragueneau:

How to make almond tarts

Beat, until it mercy begs,

Two dozen eggs.

---

136 Mrs. Beeton, Isabella *The Book of Household Management*, S. O. Beeton in 24 Monthly Parts 1859-1861. First Published in a Bound Edition 1861.

When the consistency's like silk

Add a cup of lemon juice,

Then introduce

Two tablespoons of almond milk.

Layer the patty-cans to taste

With custard paste:

Then, with clean hand, I implore,

Make a pattern shaped like wedges

Round the edges.

Now the time has come to pour

In the pans your preparation

With great elation

Insert in oven, medium heated,

Remove them when they're nicely browned.

And what is found?

The tarts all ready to be eaten! [137]

For the sweet-toothed, Norman Douglas' *Venus in the Kitchen* offers Eden-esque recipes, so tempting that merely the words would set one salivating. Two which caught my eye were **Marmalade of Carnations** (a mix of sugar, water and carnations crushed, pulped and boiled) and **Pistachio**

[137] Rostand, Edmund, translated by Christopher Fry *Cyrano de Bergerac* Oxford University Press, USA; Reissue edition (August 31, 2009), p. 41-42

Cream (pistachio nuts, brandy, cream and two egg yolks), simply, seductively sumptuous.[138]

The Convent Serpent

Beat **six whole eggs**; add a **quarter of a pound of sugar** and **as much butter**; again flavour as you fancy with **lemon, vanilla** or **orange flower water**. Incorporate enough flour to have a thick paste. Fold and roll the paste into a round in the form of a snake. To simulate the eyes and the scales use **dried sultanas** and cover the back with **almonds** each cut into lengthwise. Let it cook in a gentle oven.[139]

Nun's farts

Put into a saucepan two large glasses of **water**, 3 spoons of **sugar** and one hundred twenty five grams of **butter**.

When the water boils little by little, allow half a pound of **flour** to drop into it, working with a wooden spoon until the paste is smooth and consistent and without lumps.

Continue to cook for ten minutes stirring continuously; take the saucepan away from the fire and when

138 Douglas, Norman *Venus in the Kitchen* Bloomsbury, 2002, p. 169
139 Lautrec Toulouse- Lautrec & Joyant, M *The Art of Cuisine* Holt Rinehart Winston, 1966, p. 151

the paste is cold mix in **six eggs**, one after the other each time beating vigorously. Flavour as you fancy with **lemon, orange, rum, orange flower** and let the paste rest for a good hour.

At the time of the meal, with a wooden spoon make well rounded nuts of the paste and let them slip into hot **frying fat**; raise the temperature of the fat as the fritters swell. In six or seven minutes, the fritters ought to be plumped up and brown. Take them out, drain them, sprinkle them lightly with sugar and serve very hot. [140]

Atteraux Victoria

– a sweet sausage

Rum-soaked, circular-cut pieces of peeled apples are threaded alternately on skewers with pieces of Christmas pudding, creating a sausage like shape. Dip in a batter then fry in hot oil. Serve with brandy butter.[141]

Strawberry breasts

A pink plate with two erect feminine breasts made out of ricotta, dyed pink with Campari, with nipples of candied strawberry, with more

140 Toulouse- Lautrec & Joyant, M *The Art of Cuisine* Holt Rinehart Winston, 1966, p. 151
141 Lucan, Medlar, Gray, Durian *The Decadent Cookbook* Dedalus, 2009, p. 155

fresh strawberries under the covering of ricotta making it possible 'to bite into an idea of a multiplication of imaginary breasts'. [142]

Ice cream is exquisite. What a pity it isn't illegal.
– Voltaire (1694-1778)

Mme Pompadour's Ice cream

Ingredients

Vanilla ice cream   Small strawberries

Sponge cake   White wine

Caster sugar   Whipping cream

Glass of Cointreau (or any other sweet liqueur as you wish)

Method

Layers of ice-cream alternate with sponge doused in liqueur, one on top of the other, allowing room for a pyramid of wine-soaked strawberries and sweetened whipped cream. An impressive sweet to be served immediately. [143]

---

142 The Futurist cookbook Tommaso Marinetti (translated by Suzanne Brill) *The Futurist Cookbook* Trefoil Publications Ltd © 1989, p. 156

143 http://www.madamedepompadour.com/_eng_pomp/galleria/ditutto/ricette.htm

It would have been shameful not to have included an asparagus recipe in this aphrodisiacal work...

Asparagus Pudding

Caramelised asparagus in a set custard - an innovative dessert which makes use of this aphrodisiac more usually eaten as a starter and may well be just the dish required to cut to the chase.[144]

Ingredients

Cooked, chopped white asparagus	Gelatine
Cream	Caster sugar
Milk	Four egg yolks
Asparagus liquid	2 thick white asparagus stalks, cooked in advance

Cheesy Kisses

'A dessert course without cheese is like a beautiful woman with one eye'
– Brillat-Savarin

In his memoirs, Casanova admits he had no choice but to abandon his pet project, a *Dictionary*

---

144 The dessert recipe of Harold van Bowen, chef at Aubergine de Kites
http://www.londonfoodfilmfiesta.co.uk/Artmaiffi1/Aphrodisiacs%20-%20Food%20to%20turn%20you%20on.htm

of Cheeses, as it would require a lifetime of work. Instead, he had to be content with using cheese to bait his pretty *mice*.

— The Morning After... —

Having made it thus far, breakfast may well be the last thing on your mind. But given time, your taste buds will require reviving and your appetite replenishing and what better than an oyster to perk you up?

'Oysters are the usual opening to a winter breakfast; indeed, they are almost indispensable' declared Grimod de la Reyniere (1758-1838). Casanova, who admitted to seducing 122 women in his memoirs, famously breakfasted on 50 oysters.

However, there is one food hard to surpass in terms of its versatility, shape-shifting and nutritional value: the humble egg.

How do like you like your eggs in the morning?
According to a tired old gag – *unfertilized.*

Otherwise, they may be taken beaten, boiled, scrambled, poached, fried, baked, or swallowed raw... and this before they have been partnered with smoked salmon, caviar, spinach, bacon, sausages, hash browns, mushrooms, baked beans, honey, jam, cream, brandy, etcetera.

Len's Eggs – shaken and stirred

1960s famous spy writer Len Deighton had huge success with his cookbook Len Deighton's Action Cook Book. Deighton was all man, i.e. a ladies' man. The cover shows him stirring up something in a pot, a gun sticking out of his pocket, with an attractive woman coming up behind him. Regarding omelettes and the making of, he offered the following advice...[145]

> Omelette making is not an art or a craft – it is a knack. If you have never made an omelette before do not be disappointed if the first time is a little unsuccessful, for like sex and smoking, it is worth persevering with. Try again.

If at first you don't succeed...

The Russian Czarina Catherine the Great (1729-1796) was one of the most notorious monarchs of all time, renowned for her legendary sexual appetite. She had many lovers, including Potemkin, and numerous one-night stands; a favourite breakfast of hers was vodka laced tea, and caviar omelette.

---

145 Deighton Len Len Deighton's Action Cook Book Harper Perennial, 2009, p. 265

The Empress Omelette[146]

Ingredients

5 organic eggs	½ a cup of beluga caviar
salt and pepper	finest smoked salmon
fresh butter	2 teaspoons of sour cream
chopped chives	Toast for two

Method

The basic rules of making an omelette apply here. Add the chives and salmon midway before the eggs have completely set, then fold over and cook to a golden brown on both sides. Spoon the caviar on just before serving. Accompanied by the toast and sour crème, bring to the table. If caviar is not to your taste, try truffles...

If eggs do not tickle your fancy well then, there's always oats to be had.

Oliver's oats – Oh so creamy
– By Dickens, they're Delicious!
'Plain gruel is one of the best breakfasts and sup-

---

146 Allende, Isabel *Aphrodite, A Memoir of the Senses* Flamingo 1998, p. 151

pers that we can recommend the national Epi-
cure.'

So wrote Dr Kitchener in his **Receipt to make
Gruel No.572.** Gruel is associated with Dickens'
Oliver Twist, a poor man's meal of watery oats.
Yet historically it was not always so and is a dish
easily converted into the more delicious sounding 'caudle' by adding a little ale, wine or brandy
with sugar. [147]

A final note to the reader:
This, I feel, is an apt place to end and I hope that,
whether you have randomly flicked, chanced
upon or devotedly read this work line by line,
your curiosity will have been aroused, your appetite whetted and desires awakened.

One last thing with respect to the health of ones
appetite (especially in matters of love, pleasure
and the pursuit of desire), may the following
words always lie, ever-ready on the tip of your
tongue:

'Please sir can I have some more...'

---

[147] Andrews,W. T. *The Cooks Oracle* Munroe and Francis,1822, p. 357

— THE END —